Just Spirituality in a Wor

Just Spirituality in a World of Faiths

BARBARA AND TOM BUTLER

MOWBRAY

Mowbray
A Cassell imprint
Wellington House
125 Strand
London
WC2R 0BB

215 Park Avenue South
New York
NY 10003

First published 1996

British Library Cataloguing-in-Publication Data
A catalogue record for this book is available from the British Library.

ISBN 0–264–67337–9

Typeset by Keystroke, Jacaranda Lodge, Wolverhampton.
Printed and bound in Great Britain by Biddles Ltd,
Guildford and King's Lynn

Contents

Acknowledgements

The author and publisher wish to thank the following for permission to reprint copyright material. Although every effort has been made to contact the owners of the copyright material reproduced in this book, it has not been possible to trace all of them. If such owners contact the publisher, the appropriate acknowledgements will appear in any future editions.

Constantine Cavafy, 'Ithaka', from *Collected Poems*, translated by Edmund Keeley and Philip Sherrard, published by The Hogarth Press, 1990. Reprinted by permission of Chatto & Windus.

T. S. Eliot, extract from *Murder in the Cathedral*, from *Complete Plays of T. S. Eliot*, published by Faber & Faber, 1964. Reprinted by permission of Faber & Faber Ltd.

Edwina Gately, 'Silent God', from *I Hear a Seed Growing*, published by Source Books, 1990. Reprinted by permission of Source Books.

Garth Hewitt, 'Ten measures of beauty', from *Palestinian Pain and Promise*, published by Christians Aware, 1992. Reprinted by permission of Nelson Word Publishing Ltd.

Philip Larkin, extract from 'Best Society', from *Collected Poems*, published by Faber & Faber, 1988. Reprinted by permission of Faber & Faber Ltd.

D. H. Lawrence, 'Thought', from *Complete Poems of D. H. Lawrence*, published by Penguin, 1977. Reprinted by permission of Laurence Pollinger and the Estate of Frieda Lawrence Ravagli.

Anthony de Mello, 'The mystic was back from the desert', from *Transcendence*, published by Westminster Interfaith, 1994. Reprinted by permission of the publisher.

Douglas Sealy, 'I Am the Wind', from *The Deer's Cry*, published by Four Courts Press, 1986. Reprinted by permission of Four Courts Press and Douglas Sealy.

Foreword

More and more, in the last twenty years or so, we have realized that to speak about justice and the struggle for justice can be a tense and even sterile business if it is divorced from the rather different kind of struggle that goes on in our own growing up as human beings before God. That second struggle has a paradox in it: how do we get to the point or the place where we can breathe more freely, where we can *receive* more freely? Without that question, we are stuck with an enormous agenda for incurable anxiety, burdened as we are with the awareness of outrages in the world on a scale we cannot pretend to solve, yet cannot ignore. Again and again the problem comes back of how we are to live honestly in the world without despair.

It is this central issue that Tom and Barbara address here. They do so from a plainly Christian perspective, yet with an equally clear consciousness of the fact that Christians are not the only people engaged with the issue. This is not a book of 'comparative religion', nor is it an argument for pluralism and indifference in relations between the world's religious traditions. All it seeks to do is to remind us that the gift of living honestly, yet without despair, is a gift that is given in countless settings, across the religious spectrum. They focus on nine different kinds of sacredness, nine contexts and complexes of images in which the costly process of living your way into a reconciled humanity is realized. We are invited to learn, not argue, here; so that this is a book that requires thoughtful and responsive reading, not a quick digesting of the main points. It speaks deeply to the imagination.

Different readers will be arrested by different images. I found specially enriching the evocation of different kinds of journeying

– nomadism, pilgrimage, marathon running; the brilliant meditation on 'chastity' as singleness of mind and heart, with all that this costs, chastity as a condition of spiritual education; the interpretation of the fundamental Hindu mantra, AUM; the haunting language of 'a load of care coming out of the blue and expanding, then through a faithful response lives being transformed' (p. 136). And, not least important, I valued the sober warnings in the last chapter about the kind of sacredness (or pseudo-sacredness) that turns into an idolatry requiring human sacrifice. Sacredness can become the game of an élite, a game that demands winners and losers, and so demands exclusions. 'Sacred cows' displace the real struggle: instead of the struggle against dehumanization and against my own compulsive slithering towards the less-than-human in my own thoughts and reactions, I adopt a struggle against a human enemy, a stranger or inferior – and so cut myself off from the power of the holy itself.

The whole of this book is about reconnecting with the strength of the holy, in such a way that our lives as well as our words and policies can be signs of justice in its fullest sense – the just and humane balance of our imaginations and feelings, as well as the balance of justice in our public life and social relations. It will be a welcome resource for all kinds of groups, and a powerful witness to the desires and the labours which human beings share across the boundaries of race and faith traditions.

Rowan Williams
Bishop of Monmouth

Introduction

THE NATURAL starting-point for religious discussion and exploration in past centuries has generally been doctrine, or religious truth. This seems to be less so in today's world, where the natural starting-point is spirituality or religious experience. This approach is similar to the way in which many people tackle their personal computer. They are more concerned about making it work than understanding how it works. This is not to say that religious truth does not matter, it does, but people are far more likely to become interested in such truth when they have had the experience of religion working, particularly during key moments in their lives.

We believe that a religion which is to work today must bring together awareness of the profound mystery and wonder of life and awareness of practical and everyday living. It therefore avoids a mysticism which loses contact with day-to-day life and a humanism which reduces people to mere physical beings. Religion, then, is to be tested by its relevance to the world's experience and understanding of life, and also by its capacity to embody the profound dimension of humanness. Its myths, rites and symbols are powerfully effective inasmuch as they provide a vehicle for getting in touch with human depths and a sense of the holy, and at the same time give believers confidence and encouragement in the worldly challenges of life and death. Religion is both an inevitable part of human society and the means by which that society relates to the most profound questions of its life.

Spirituality lies at the heart of religion. It is the way in which people in all times and places encounter the holiness, the mystery, the fear and fascination of existence, of their own life and death, and of their calling to be members of their family, their tribe, their

I

nation, their species, their world. Spirituality, poetically, might be described as a fall through ordinary life into the depths of life.

It might be instructive to remind ourselves that in the New Testament record the encounter with holiness did not so much lead to the feeling of numinous, as when the hair on the back of the neck stands up, but more to the catching of the breath in wonder. Neither was holiness the opposite of the profane or mundane. The writers showed little interest in 'holy' people, clothes, objects, or places. On the contrary, to the New Testament writers, holiness was encountered in unexpected ways in the midst of ordinary life. Following Jesus was to live in the same world as usual but to see it in a totally different way; as though wearing spectacles for the first time, a blurred world suddenly became clear.

Loren Eiseley tells how one very foggy day a man was cautiously making his way along the path across a field which lay between his house and the railway station when he was startled by a seemingly enormous bird swooping past his face. As the bird went by it gave a loud cry of terror. When he had recovered his composure the man realized that the bird was indeed a large crow which often inhabited a high tree in the neighbourhood, but he was puzzled that such a bird had been so shaken by the encounter. Then he realized that the fog had brought the clouds down to touch the earth so that the world of the earth and the world of the sky had overlapped. The crow, of course, had not been aware of this and had thought that it was flying through the clouds, high above the earth, when it had encountered the totally unexpected sight of what appeared to be a sky-walking man. No wonder the bird had been so shaken; it had learned that life on the overlap is frequently surprising and challenging.[1]

The spiritual journey is a journey through life on the overlap, the overlap between the ordinary and the profound, the down-to-earth and the holy. Embarking upon the journey, then, does not imply a disengagement from ordinary life. The return from 'the holy' to 'the ordinary world' is part of the classic religious journey of humanity. Isaiah was told by the Lord in the awe-filled temple to go and speak to a people who would not hear him, and Isaiah went forth. Jesus left the mountain of the Transfiguration, despite the pleas of his closest disciples, and resumed the journey to Jerusalem, where he would confront the leaders of church and state. The Buddha journeyed to Nirvana and then according to one tradition came back to the world so that suffering people might profit from the illumination which he had discovered. The pilgrim who returns from 'the holy' to 'the ordinary' is both the same and different: the same, because he or she is living in the same world as everybody else; different, because, like the crow, an added dimension of experience and understanding has occurred.

Our generation is particularly fortunate in having the faith stories and experiences of the whole world available for consideration. The Buddha is reported to have said that his teachings were but a handful of leaves taken from all the leaves in the forest. In spirituality we believe that it is important for people to focus, at least at first, on the handful of leaves which comes from their own culture and faith, and to live in the light of its illumination – our way to God is usually also God's way to us. But whilst we honour and respect our own handful of leaves we should also be aware that the forest of God is full of leaves of great beauty and strength and that others also walk there.

This book is an attempt to begin to share our walk through a larger forest of God than is sometimes encountered. Our ministries have taken us to different parts of the world and have brought us deep friendships with people of many cultures in our own land. This is our personal spiritual account and by no means a rigorous study of differing faiths or cultures. It is our experience that 'life on the overlap' can be spiritually enriching, whilst one's faith and understanding of one's own religion can be deepened and enhanced. Common themes and images of spirituality appear and reappear in different times and places and we will be visiting some of these themes in this book: the sacred journey, the sacred mountain, the sacred land; the silence of the desert, the sacred community; worship, suffering and work. And just because of the profound nature of spirituality, its shadow can be powerfully destructive and so we also consider 'sacred cows' – what can happen when spirituality goes wrong.

NOTE

1.   L. Eiseley, *The Immense Journey* (Garnstone Press, London, 1957).

CHAPTER ONE

Sacred Journeys

ITHAKA

As you set out for Ithaka
hope your road is a long one,
full of adventure, full of discovery.
Laistrygonians, Cyclops,
angry Poseidon – don't be afraid of them:
you'll never find things like that on your way
as long as you keep your thoughts raised high,
as long as a rare excitement
stirs your spirit and your body.
Laistrygonians, Cyclops,
wild Poseidon – you won't encounter them
unless you bring them along inside your soul,
unless your soul sets them up in front of you.

Hope your road is a long one.
May there be many summer mornings when,
with what pleasure, what joy,
you enter harbours you're seeing for the first time;
may you stop at Phoenician trading stations
to buy fine things,
mother of pearl and coral, amber and ebony,
sensual perfume of every kind –
as many sensual perfumes as you can;
and may you visit many Egyptian cities
to learn and go on learning from their scholars.

Keep Ithaka always in your mind.
Arriving there is what you're destined for.
But don't hurry the journey at all.
Better if it lasts for years,
so you're old by the time you reach the island,
wealthy with all you've gained on the way,
not expecting Ithaka to make you rich.

Constantine Cavafy

There is a Jewish story about a group of travellers who become lost in a thick forest. They come across a rabbi who has been lost for even longer. Unaware of his helplessness they ask him to show them the way out of the forest. He answers, 'That I cannot do. But I can point out the way that leads further into the forest, and after that let us find the way together.'[1] Perhaps the commonest image of the spiritual life in all faith traditions is the image of the journey – of finding the way together. This is understandable because the human race is a species forever engaged in journeying. From its origins in Africa humankind has now spread to every continent on earth. Nomadic people still move their herds around huge tracts of land, setting up temporary homes and then moving on. The Maasai people in East Africa roam around between Kenya and Tanzania with their three million or so cattle, which they believe were sent to earth by God. Cattle herding is the all-important work of the Maasai, and almost everything they have and eat comes from the cow or from sheep or goats. Even the simple houses or *manyatta* are made of twigs and mud and cow dung. The houses easily collapse when the people move on to new places, usually in search of green pastures for the cattle. The Maasai walk for long distances daily, hunting, herding, gathering wood and water. After Tanzania achieved independence a law aimed at the Maasai was passed, that male bus passengers should wear trousers. The Maasai were mostly unaware of, and therefore untroubled by, the new law. They continued proudly to wear their traditional dress, and to walk everywhere.

The Maasai, like nomadic people the world over, journey because it is their natural way of life. Some people have journeys thrust upon them because of the pressures of war, famine or disease. When Alan Bennett was a child of five, World War II broke out and his home city of Leeds was threatened with air-raids. His parents took him and his brother down to the bus station to wait for a bus going anywhere out of the now-dangerous city. After a long wait a bus bound for Pately Bridge arrived, and the family got onto it. They alighted in a small village in Nidderdale and his father, a shy man, bravely requested shelter at a farm opposite the bus stop. The family was taken in and father returned to Leeds.[2]

The world's refugees are not always so fortunate. They face

many and mostly unpleasant surprises in their unsought-for journeys in the face of war or natural disasters, not knowing where the future will lie or what it will bring. We visited Vietnamese people in their detention camps in the New Territories of Hong Kong. A vision of a more fulfilling way of life had caused them to risk the dangers of sea and pirates and now they waited in the hope of travelling on to America, Australia or Europe. In the corners of their barn-like buildings they had created religious shrines containing precious images brought with them on their hazardous journeys. Such objects linked them with their past whilst also holding forth the hope of a richer future. The spiritual image of the journey in the faith traditions carries similar links and hopes.

There is one journey which all human beings share with every creature – the journey from birth, through life, to death. Different faiths and traditions may speculate and disagree upon the reality and nature of life before birth or after death, but all agree that life is a significant journey which is to be taken with the uttermost seriousness.

Of course the speculation concerning life before birth or after death does affect the way in which the journey between birth and death is tackled. A good Hindu friend of ours, when we were becoming rather agitated about a particularly pressing problem, said to us, 'Calm down, there is plenty of time – innumerable incarnations.' And if your belief is that there are innumerable incarnations, then it will affect the way you live your life. Not every injustice needs to be tackled now – there are innumerable incarnations in which to deal with the problem. Not every personal weakness need be a cause for regret or despair – in this incarnation simply try to make progress in one area of weakness, there are innumerable incarnations in which to tackle the others. This is perhaps the reason why those Eastern societies influenced particularly by Buddhism and Hinduism have traditionally been more relaxed and tolerant about some social problems. They have also been less intrusive into the world of nature – seeing a continuity in all life, rather than analysing life into components the better to change it.

The Christian tradition, together with Judaism and Islam, has seen each human life as a one-off, never-to-be-repeated event, preparing for, or rehearsing, a more perfect life to come after death. In this tradition each individual's life is to be taken with the uttermost seriousness, because it is a unique gift from God. One of the shocks to which every individual comes, and then tends to forget, is the fact that no one is designed to live for ever, and death is thus virtually the one certainty in life. This realization can bring terror, but it can also bring the determination to live life to the full. Societies like those in the West which have been influenced by these traditions tend therefore to be purposeful and forward-looking and to place a great emphasis upon problem-solving. A possible consequence of this is an attitude which sees the natural world as the raw material for building a richer life for humanity. We will explore in a later chapter the experience of our own times, when the worlds of East and West are meeting in dialogue just as the Western approach to nature is threatening to poison the planet by its very 'success'.

Whether one sees the life between birth and death as one of innumerable incarnations or as a one-off, never-to-be-repeated happening, however, the journey is a good image to use to describe the experience. In the Eastern tradition the journey has the form of a spiral, with each turn in the spiral relating to a particular incarnation, but nevertheless moving the self forward on an axis pointing to a more perfect future. In the Christian tradition the journey is more like the flight of an arrow shooting forward into an unknown future.

The archetypal journey in the Jewish and Christian traditions, of course, is the Exodus related in the fourteenth and following chapters of the Book of Exodus. The people of Israel believed that they were freed from their slavery in Egypt by a mighty act of God. They were promised a holy and fulfilling future in their own land and they spent a lifetime journeying towards that land. The journey took them through deserts and dangers and past mountains made holy for them by their encounters with God. The people of Israel and Moses did not always have the same attitude to the journey. To Moses the journey was a pilgrimage; to the people of Israel it was often pure purgatory, a time of hunger and thirst, of confusion and desolation, of fear and anxiety. They started their journey as a slave rabble and at times they looked back with longing to their slavery in Egypt, yet they ended their journey as a people in covenant with God, knowing who they were, where they were going, and what their purpose was in life. For their journey gave them the opportunity to wrestle with God, to understand something of God's character, to learn the demands God makes upon his people, and by so doing to grow in maturity and holiness. We will examine in later chapters some of the ingredients of this journey, including the mountain, the desert, the suffering and the community, but here we want to stay with the journey itself.

A further image of journey which influenced the Christian tradition, at least in part, is Plato's picture of people journeying out of the cave of illusion into the light of reality. In this well-known picture, the people in the dark cave are in a rather different form of slavery to the people of Israel in Egypt – they are in slavery to illusion because they believe the flickering shadows cast on the cave wall from the fire are real figures. It is only when they journey to the cave mouth and stand in the sunlight that their eyes are opened to true reality. So, this tradition has it, the human challenge is to travel through the dark cave of illusion, illumined merely by the light of the fires of our own emotions, hopes and dreams, whose walls are peopled by shadows of our own imaginings; to travel out of this cave of illusion into the light of reality where, with open eyes, we can see things as they truly are. The Hindu saying, 'Lead me from the unreal to the real; lead me from darkness to light; lead me from death to immortality',[3] has echoes of this imagery.

The spiritual journey is not merely a journey from darkness to light, from illusion to reality; it is also a journey from falsehood to truth, from evil to good. It is a journey which can involve pain and purging because to leave some of our cherished illusions behind requires a painful reorientating of our lives. When a new convert is baptized in the Christian tradition or reaffirms baptismal promises in the service of Confirmation, the first question asked is, 'Do you turn to Christ?' and only when the answer 'I turn to Christ' is received can the service of initiation proceed. The pilgrim has turned around and is prepared to move out of the cave of personal illusion to the light of the truth of Jesus Christ – believed by Christians to be the reality of God.

The journey of initiation shows up in other traditions. Boys in most African tribes traditionally become men when they are circumcised after a lengthy preparation, isolated with their peer group from the rest of the tribe. During this painful time of initiation the secrets and traditions of the tribe are passed on to the new warrior. Nelson Mandela tells how at the age of sixteen he was initiated through the Xhosa tradition of circumcision.[4] In that tradition it was necessary to perform a daring exploit before the ceremony. In Nelson Mandela's case, he and his companions decided to steal a pig by first enticing it along a trail scented with strong beer. On the day following this exploit he and twenty-five of his companions were taken to two huts in a secluded valley, and then for a sacred time they were taught the tribal customs and made ready for the transition from boyhood to manhood.

The night before the circumcision women came from near-by villages and there was singing and dancing. At dawn the preparations began. The boys first went through a ceremony of purification, bathing in the river. At midday, clad only in blankets, they were commanded to stand in a row in front of a crowd of relatives and elders. Then they were told to sit with legs spread out in front of them. Circumcision, as well as being a ceremony of initiation, is also a trial of bravery, for no anaesthetic is used and flinching or crying out is regarded as being unmanly. The circumcision was performed by an expert wielding an assegai. As each boy was dealt with he cried out '*Ndiyindoda*' (I am a man!). He was given a circumcision name, which to the traditionalist is more acceptable than the previous given names.

Immediately after the blow had been delivered an assistant took the foreskin and tied it to a corner of the blanket and the wound was dressed with a healing plant. At the conclusion of the ceremony the new men returned to their huts where a fire burning with wet wood cast off clouds of smoke which were thought to promote healing. They were looked after by a guardian who first painted them head to foot in white ochre, symbolizing purity. Then at midnight they were taken out, one by one, to bury their foreskin, and by so doing symbolically to bury their youth. Whilst the wounds healed they continued to live in the huts, in a period of spiritual preparation for the journey of manhood which lay ahead. On the day of their emergence they went down to the river early to wash away the white ochre and then when they were clean and dry they were coated in red ochre. The huts were burned and in a great ceremony of speeches, singing, dancing, gift-giving and feasting they were welcomed as warriors into their society. Traditionally there are equivalent initiation ceremonies for girls, even in some cases circumcision ceremonies, but this practice is now dying out in many African tribes.

In the Hindu faith-tradition the growing boys journey through the Upanyan ceremony when the sacred thread is placed on their shoulders, following which the boys are allowed to participate in significant sacred ceremonies and traditions. The bar mitzvah is the Jewish ceremony marking the moment when Jewish boys religiously become men. The boys will have attended a course of preparation for this great moment in life when they are allowed to read from the Torah for the first time. Family and friends mark the occasion with a celebratory party, demonstrating that this is no mere personal pilgrimage. Although similar events called bat mitzvah can be held for girls, these are less common. This may be because women's responsibilities are more central and more obvious than those of men, undertaken naturally and therefore without the need of a special ceremony!

Tolstoy in his great work *War and Peace* described the journey of initiation which Pierre had to take when he sought to join a Mason-like order. The rituals were complex and semi-mystical with particular rituals corresponding to particular disciplines which the adherent needed to learn. It was explained that there were seven virtues including discretion, obedience and morality corresponding to the seven steps of Solomon's temple. Pierre was told that the order had a great task – the handing-on to posterity of an important mystery which had come down from ancient time – but nobody could know or profit by it unless prepared by long and diligent self-purification and enlightenment of mind. But by doing this for the sake of receiving and understanding the mystery, the brethren of the order also presented to the world an example of piety and virtue, and played their part in combating the evil in the world.[5]

This multi-sided nature of the spiritual journey was illustrated for us in a rather more down-to-earth way recently when we took part in a special journey – the London Marathon. Neither of us had run before, although we have always done a great deal of hill-walking, but we were persuaded to run as a team to help raise money for our favourite charities. The marathon was both a wonderful and a painful experience which taught us a great deal about ourselves and other people, and some of the lessons perhaps apply to the spiritual journey.

One lesson is that preparation is everything. 'Before a king goes to war,' Luke quotes Jesus as saying, 'He would be wise to count the cost.' We started training for an April marathon in January. It was nowhere near early enough. We set aside an hour a day and a half-day a week for walking, jogging and running, the theory being that we would build up gradually to long-distance running. It was a good theory but took no account of injuries – sprains, pulled muscles and other horrors which inevitably come the way of inexperienced performers.

We were like the seed in the parable of the sower, which at first grew with enthusiasm on stony soil but then wilted in the sun. We soon wilted in the dark, cold, winter mornings, running around the park. We were frustrated by pulled calf-muscles. It is not unknown for religious folk to approach their spiritual journeys with the same enthusiasm. Perhaps a sermon, or book, or retreat has planted a great desire in their hearts to go out and progress in prayer, in meditation and discipleship and off they go, soon to be brought low by the equivalent of dark, cold mornings and pulled calf-muscles. Those are times of prayer when no heart is warmed, no response is felt and one's words and prayers seem merely to be going into a great void of indifference. No wonder so many competitors never even reach the marathon starting-line – the months of preparation are a solitary marathon in themselves.

Despite the frustration, however, we found ourselves on a breezy April Sunday morning on Blackheath Common with thirty thousand or so other runners waiting for the starting-gun. We soon discovered that there were three sorts of people participating in the event. Firstly, there were the joggers, just there for the run, happy to be participating, enjoying the company and the occasion, jogging along merrily in the sun-shine, not worrying at all about their finishing time, but hoping to reach the end of the journey eventually.

Secondly there were the ambitious competitors – out to win or to improve upon their previous personal best time. Then thirdly there were those who were running for others – whose journey, whatever the time of finishing, was aiding some good cause. These folk came in all shapes and sizes and in all costumes – ostriches, whales, police officers, nurses, jugglers and clowns. The spiritual life is equally a marathon of faith embarked upon by similar groups of people. At different times on our journey of faith we show up maybe in different ways. Sometimes we are happy just to be the spiritual joggers – reading our Bibles, praying our prayers, joining with others in worship. At such times we are grateful for any insights we might receive, any uplifting thoughts or emotions, but we do not expect to be over-challenged or exerted.

This, of course, would not have been good enough for the apostle Paul. In his first letter to the Corinthians (1 Cor 9.24) he told his readers that Christians were like runners in the games, and that they were to run to win a garland that never fades. St Paul then challenged us on our journey of faith to be more like the second group of people in the marathon, the ambitious competitors – those who constantly remember what the race is for. There may be no place for personal ambition in the journey of faith, but there are ways in which ambition is right and proper, including the ambition to ever widen and deepen one's spiritual understanding, the ambition to journey more into the life of prayer and devotion, the ambition for one's soul to be touched occasionally by the wonder of heaven, and the ambition for the world to be changed through the grace of God and the energy and dedication of those seeking to follow the teachings of God.

And at times we are challenged to be more like the third group of people taking part in the marathon – those who run for others. The spiritual life cannot merely be a course in self-improvement, or another aesthetic experience. At times we shall merely jog along. At times we shall have great insights and experiences, but if we are to journey healthily we must never forget for long that ours is a journey with God, to God, and for the good of the world of God.

There have been times and places in the history of humankind where the reality of God has seemed particularly close. At such times and in such places humankind has often taken a new direction in its spiritual journey, or has changed gear in its spiritual commitment.

For example, a time of special awareness of God for a large part of the world was the time around 500 BCE. Both overland and by sea the trade routes between the great civilizations were opened up and developed and as a consequence there was a great exchange of cultural and religious ideas. Second Isaiah was bringing hope to the Jewish people in exile in Babylon; the *Bhagavad Gita*, 'the glory of Sanskrit literature', was enriching Hinduism; the Buddha was seeking Nirvana; Mahavira was re-founding the Jain faith; whilst Athens saw the birth of Plato, the first thinker to write systematically on the subject of politics.

There was an equivalent period of great spiritual resurgence in the years between 1 and 500 CE. During this time, following the life of Jesus Christ, the Christian religion was born and the Church developed its doctrines and selected the canon of sacred scripture. A similar process of reflection and selection took place in Judaism following the destruction of the temple at Jerusalem during the war with the Romans in 70 CE. Gnosticism, a strange mystical amalgam of Western and Eastern religious concepts, blossomed and weakened, and at the other end of the globe Buddhism entered China on its way to Japan, where it would develop in fresh ways including the remarkable tradition of Zen Buddhism.

The places where new faith was born or old faith renewed tended to become sacred places to their adherents – centres of pilgrimage, symbols of yearning for a richer, purer, more meaningful life. Many have felt sanctity in the stones; the prayers of countless pilgrims have made the air holy; visiting the sites has led to an ascension of the mind and heart. The holy place becomes the centre of a holy landscape, which in some manner maps out the meeting between the world and the divine.

> For the blood of Thy martyrs and saints
> Shall enrich the earth, shall create the holy places.
> For wherever a saint has dwelt, wherever a martyr has given
> his blood for the blood of Christ,
> There is holy ground, and the sanctity shall not depart from it
> Though armies trample over it, though sightseers come with
> guide-books looking over it;
>
> T. S. Eliot[6]

Jerusalem is a holy place and centre of pilgrimage for Jews, Christians and Muslims, which makes it a very special place and also a very troubled place. To believers it has been a place where sacred history has touched human history. Jerusalem is one of Islam's three most holy places. The Dome of the Rock marks the spot where, Muslims believe, the Prophet Muhammad was carried by God into Paradise. Christians have been present in Jerusalem ever since the crucifixion and resurrection of Jesus. Palestinian Christians today talk of their sense of responsibility in living and keeping alive the Christian faith in the land where the Church was born and in Jerusalem, 'The Mother of All Churches'. The attachment of the churches of the Orthodox East to the Holy City is particularly deep and vivid, but the Church of the Holy Sepulchre, for example, is shared by many Christian denominations.[7]

For the Jewish people the Western Wall has been the focus for their tears – tears of pain, and tears of expectation. Like the city, the wall is a hybrid. It consists of several layers of stone blocks. The oldest stem from Herod's temple, built in the last century before Jesus and in its time one of the wonders of the world. Its white marble glistens from afar in the sunlight like a snow-covered mountain. In the Jewish uprising against the Romans in 70 CE the temple was occupied by Zealot fighters and was virtually razed to the ground. The wall today includes four rows of smaller stones added by the Romans as they converted the temple into a citadel. On top of this are several more layers added by the Muslims between 700 and 1200 CE. The Western Wall thus encapsulates the history, the pride and the tragedy of the Jewish people.

> Ten measures of beauty God gave to the world,
> Nine to Jerusalem, one to the rest.
> Ten measures of sorrow God gave to the world,
> Nine to Jerusalem, one to the rest.
>
> Garth Hewitt[8]

In the Christian tradition the tombs of the martyrs in Rome became revered holy places, and Christians would gather there particularly on their 'heavenly birthdays', the anniversaries of their martyrdom. Church buildings where the relics of the saint occupied a central place were created over the tomb and became centres of pilgrimage. From this developed the practice of churches everywhere being associated with local saints and martyrs and having holy relics as a focus of devotion.

Canterbury has been a place of pilgrimage, prayer, poetry and art for Christians since Thomas Becket was martyred in the twelfth century for standing up for the things of God against the might of the state. The cathedral grew as the numbers of pilgrims grew throughout the Middle Ages. The centre of pilgrimage was the tomb of Becket beyond the high altar of the cathedral and the chair of St Augustine where successive Archbishops of Canterbury are enthroned. Beautiful coloured light filters into the cathedral through the ancient stained-glass windows containing pictures which illustrate stories of healing attributed to St Thomas. As grateful pilgrims offered their gifts the tomb became a treasury. Perhaps not surprisingly, that treasury became the first target of the king's soldiers at the Reformation, and the bones of the martyr disappeared together with cart-loads of booty.

Nothing remains of the tomb or the treasury today, but the sacred structure of the great cathedral was influenced by it, and the magnificent building still moves hearts and uplifts souls. The enormous crypt, built to hold up the sanctuary and tower, has carvings around the massive pillars reminding one of images in a dream. As pilgrims today sit or pray in the crypt chapels it is as though they are visiting the 'unconscious' of the cathedral, whilst as they walk through the lengthy nave with its tall pillars and interlocking tracery forming the roof, it is as though they are walking through a holy forest.

If a great medieval cathedral has echoes of a holy forest, a mosque has echoes of a sacred oasis, surely appropriate for the desert people from whom Islam has its origins. Everywhere Islam spread, its adherents built mosques as earthly hints of what they believed paradise might be: mosques whose architecture reminded them of the swaying palm trees, the shade and splash of light and shadow imaging the sparkle of running water. Although Muslims often say, 'The whole world is a mosque', yet, like those of other faith-traditions, they have felt the need to build holy buildings where they are particularly reminded of the presence and claims of the holy God. The mosque in Arabic is known as the *masjid*, the place of prostration. In it there is no furniture or image, for nothing must detract from the worship of God, but simply a carpeted floor where those who pray stand united in humility and equality.

Every Muslim has to go to Mecca at least once in his or her lifetime if they are able, and the pilgrimage, '*Hajj*', is planned sometimes for many years. Pilgrims wear only two seamless sheets of white cotton to remind them that, rich or poor, all are alike in the sight of God. Each day of the pilgrimage has its own special rituals which recall incidents in the ministry of the prophet Muhammad. The whole pilgrimage is focused around the Ka'aba, a cuboid of a building 40 by 35 by 50 feet, draped in black brocade with the woven gold lettering, 'No God but Allah. And Muhammad, his Prophet.' Its four corners point to the four points of the compass. Inside the Ka'aba? Very little – three pillars to support the roof, silver and gold hanging lamps, incense and flickering shadows – and silence, in which can be heard more than can be heard. As the pilgrims wind round and round it is as though they are following the century-long journey of Islam. Here it started. 'You ride for Paradise, O Muslims,' wrote the Prophet, 'Believers! Make paradise here. Die and live in paradise for the eternal now.' And they rode out and changed their world.

In Kandy in Sri Lanka we visited a place holy to the Buddhist tradition, the Dalada Maligawa, the palace of the tooth relic. It is surrounded by a walled moat, and has stone-pillared verandahs. Its new golden roof crowns an ornately-decorated building. The 'Temple of the Tooth', as it is popularly known, is a famous place of pilgrimage where, to the beat of the drums, pilgrims offer flowers and view the golden casket which houses the tooth of the Buddha brought to Sri Lanka hidden in the hair of an Indian princess in the fourth century. At the time of the Perahera Festival in late July, processions of elephants, musicians and dancers move from the Temple of the Tooth through the streets of Kandy. The large elephant which carries a replica of the casket housing the tooth relic walks on a white carpet whilst the drummers beat furiously and the dancers move to the beat in clouds of incense.

Throughout Sri Lanka there are innumerable beautiful temples whose *dagobas*, shaped rather like bells resting on the ground, contain relics of the Buddha. At Ananadrhapura, the capital of Sri Lanka for fourteen hundred years, from the fourth century BCE, 'the oldest tree in the world' is a focus for pilgrimage, because it is the Bodhi-tree, said to be a sapling of the tree under which the Buddha gained enlightenment.

Amritsar in India is a city holy to the people of the Sikh faith. It was founded by the fourth Guru, Guru Ram Das. The Guru had a pool created there when the land was given to the Sikhs, and a city grew around it. The fifth Guru then had a temple built in the middle of the pool. Four entrances were made to show that all peoples, from all four castes of Indian society and from the four points of the compass, were welcome. Over the years it has been rebuilt and re-embellished with gold and precious stones so that it has become known as the Golden Temple. The temple contains some of the earliest copies of the Guru Granth Sahib, the holy book of the Sikhs, which is continuously read through from beginning to end all day within the golden temple whilst the pilgrims pour in, having first bathed in the pool around the temple. Around the world Sikhs gather in worship and community at the gurdwara, meaning 'the door of the Guru'. Sikhs believe that the holy book, the Guru Granth Sahib, is their Guru, and this holy book is central to their worship and the only object which is venerated. Any member of the congregation may read from it during the services.

As well as the exterior journeys – the journeys to places of pilgrimage – there is, perhaps even more significantly, and certainly involving far more people, the interior journey, the journey which people make when they reflect, meditate or pray. It is this journey which people strive to make when they spend days or even weeks at retreat houses, and never was there a time when going on retreat was more popular. This might be a reaction to the stressful nature of modern life, but equally it might well reflect the deep desire which many feel to find meaning and purpose in their lives. This journey is not to the sacred place, but it is a journey to find and befriend the sacred centre within, the place which is everywhere and nowhere, centre and circumference, the centre which in Christian tradition is known as the soul.

This journey can be as arduous and demanding as any external pilgrimage, for like an onion the human person is made up of many different levels, and to start journeying beyond the most familiar and obvious outer person can be disturbing. Hermann Hesse, in his short novel *The Journey to the East*, speaks of a league made up of a procession of believers and disciples 'incessantly . . . moving towards the East, towards the Home of

Light'.[9] But it also becomes clear that the league is within, as is the two-billion-year-old historical archive which tells of its story – the human brain.

The members of the league in the novel start on their quest for many and various reasons – boredom, treasure-seeking, desire for certainty, to find a beautiful princess, as well as more secret and lofty aims, but during his year's novitiate the narrator hears a phrase which pleases him and gives him courage later: 'Where are we really going? Always home.' At first all goes well. They visit sacred places, honour former saints, and though often mocked by unbelievers they travel with a feeling of unity and purpose. They see wonders with their own eyes. They listen to new legends. Yet they are warned that:

> He who travels far will often see things
> Far removed from what he believed was Truth.
> When he talks about it in the field at home,
> He is often accused of lying.

Soon things go wrong. One of the travellers begins to have doubts about the worth of the journey. He is told by the leader, 'You have said goodbye to us and want to return to common sense and useful work. You are absolved from your vow.' 'Also from the vow of silence?' cries the deserter. 'Yes also from the vow of silence,' answers the leader. 'You vowed to keep silent about the secret of the League to unbelievers. As we see you have forgotten the secret, you will not be able to pass it on to anyone.'

So the young man leaves. Then he changes his mind and tries to rejoin, but his quest is in vain. The other travellers hear of his desire to rejoin them and plead with their leader to forgive his disloyalty. The leader answers:

We should be happy if he did find his way back to us, but we cannot help him. I fear that he would not see and recognize us even if we passed close by him; he has become blind. A similar thing has happened to many other people. Once in their youth the light shone for them; they saw the light and followed the star, but then came reason and the mockery of the world; then came weariness and disillusion, and so they lost their way again, they became blind once more. Some of them have spent the rest of their lives looking for us again, but could not find us. They have then told the world that our League is only a pretty legend and people should not be misled by it. Others have become our deadly enemies and have abused and harmed the League in every possible way.

This experience of losing the way and becoming blind to the presence of the league becomes the narrator's experience, and the bulk of the novel is spent describing his pain and unfulfilment. He repents his unfaithfulness, but 'Repentance alone does not help. Grace cannot be bought with repentance; it cannot be bought at all.'

This remarkable story contains within it many of the ingredients which are commonly experienced in the spiritual journey – the dissatisfaction with the dullness of ordinary life, the glimpse of light and meaning, the learning of sacred languages and truths, the prayers and promises, the feeling of hope, unity, and wholeness. And then the 'magic' no longer works to the same extent, so either fanaticism or doubt, or both, creep in. What follows is disconnection with the sacred community, the turning aside from the quest, then either the yearning to return and the frustration that things are never the same again, for doubts once entertained cannot be forgotten, or hostility to the whole enterprise and particularly to those who would encourage others to pursue it. Or more commonly there is the endless seeking after new leagues, new gurus, new traditions, or new spiritual methods. And so the journey is everlasting, and, like that of Moses, although glimpses of the promised land are seen, death intervenes before it is reached.

But there is a story of a well-known journey of faith which is less pessimistic. In this story there were not three wise men who followed the star to the stable at Bethlehem but four. The fourth lost contact with his companions almost from the very start of the journey, when he turned aside to care for a sick beggar his horse had stumbled over.

By the time he arrived in Bethlehem his companions had been and gone, and so had the holy family. Whilst he was conducting his enquiries in Bethlehem, Herod's soldiers arrived and the slaughter of the innocents began. The fourth wise man did what he could to save the children and then set off to seek the holy family, scouring refugee camps everywhere. Meanwhile his companions had returned home to live with their memories of the star and the stable and the divine king. But the fourth wise man's journey never ended, for he never went home again. And although he never knelt before the holy child, he knelt beside the bed of many a sick child, many a dying adult – and caring for them became the purpose and end of his journey. Whether he had reached his goal he never had time to ask, since he was too busy and fulfilled in the tasks of care on hand.

A powerful African portrayal of the nativity is to be found in Murang'a Cathedral in Central Kenya. In the cathedral there are murals of the gospel stories seen through Gikuyu culture. One of the murals depicts the birth of Jesus in the setting of the Kenyan Emergency in the early 1950s. This was the time when people who did not sign the oath to support the Mau Mau guerillas were in danger of losing their lives. Most Christians did not take the oath, because it involved promising to bring change by fighting and killing, and many were themselves killed. During this time the colonial authorities imposed a curfew, the villages were fenced off and people ordered to stay within them. The mural of the birth of Jesus shows a fenced-off village, and, a long way away, on top of a hill, the African hut with the new-born baby and his mother. In between the village and the hut there is dense forest, with the danger of robbers, animals and, at the time of the mural, capture by the authorities or death at the hands of the Mau Mau. Down in one corner of the mural are three figures, leaving the village to go on the dangerous journey to take gifts to the new baby. The three figures are three wise women, because men would never visit a new baby in the Gikuyu cultural setting.

We will return to the theme of the sacred task later, but perhaps through visiting some of these examples of sacred journeys we begin to understand why a straightforward journey from Egypt to Canaan in the biblical story of the Exodus lasted for forty years. It seems that whatever we might believe to be the goal of our spiritual journey, and whatever the path to reach that goal, we must expect false starts, diversions, confusions and doubts. We must expect the journey to change its nature, and perhaps even the goal to become less significant than the way in which it is approached, for the journey, if it is authentic, is a journey away from the familiar parts of ourselves and our world, to the mysterious reality of God's call.

The popular book *The Lord of the Rings* by J.R.R. Tolkien has the homely hobbit Frodo as its unlikely hero.[10] His adventures start when he is recruited to go on a great journey whose purpose is to wrest the ring of power from those who would use it for evil

purposes. But Frodo instinctively knows that the journey will be
demanding and costly.

All the council sat with downcast eyes, as if in deep thought. A great dread
fell on him [Frodo], as if he was awaiting the pronouncement of some
doom that he had long foreseen and vainly hoped might after all never be
spoken. An overwhelming longing to rest and remain at peace by Bilbo's
side in Rivendell filled all his heart. At last with an effort he spoke, and
wondered to hear his own words, as if some other will was using his small
voice. 'I will take the ring', he said, 'though I do not know the way.'

A similar sense of dread must often have filled the heart of
Abraham, one of the earliest of the biblical travellers, on his
journey around the Fertile Crescent, a journey which at times
must have felt like a wild-goose chase. He was living his
ordinary, taken-for-granted life, back home in Ur, when the
finger of God first beckoned him and he journeyed out, not
perhaps realizing that this was to be a life-long pilgrimage.
Every time he rested and stopped and tried to put down roots
that relentless finger was there beckoning. 'But what of the
future?' At times it must have seemed that there was to be no
future. 'What of his family and descendants?' At times it must
have seemed that there were to be no descendants.

One by one the doors of possibility closed for him and shut
firmly, until it became clear that there was only one future, one
hope, his son Isaac, the gift of God to Sarah and Abraham in
their old age. And then that relentless finger of God beckoned
Abraham up the mountain with Isaac, and in horror Abraham
understood that Isaac was demanded also, and the only hope
was in the finger of God itself; the beckoning finger that had
been the cause of his journey was to be the end of his pilgrimage.

So it was for Abraham and so it was perhaps with Jesus himself. First the relaxed, open ministry in Galilee – the teaching,
the healing, the preaching, the crowds, the enthusiasm, the
gathering group of disciples crowding around; then the finger
of his heavenly Father beckoning to Jerusalem and to hostility
and danger and complexity; then the same finger beckoning
to the temple, and the garden of Gethsemane, to Pilate's palace
and gaol, to the cross and the tomb.

The journey of the life and work of Jesus from Nazareth has
been expressed poetically by Najwa Farah, a Palestinian
Christian who was born and brought up in Nazareth and

whose own life has taken her from World War II, when she saw cities attacked and occupied and villages wiped out, to the West Bank and through the Six Day War in June 1967, to Beirut and long years of continuous war, including the 1982 Israeli invasion and siege.

JESUS FROM NAZARETH

How lovely, how free
Are those walks to the hill-top
on a summer day.
The moon seemed to come down on the hill-top
faint at even-tide,
and I foolishly would run after it
aware as I ran of footsteps long ago
of him whom I love,
my friend and teacher.

There I see the lilies of the field,
the anemone and cyclamen,
the fragrance of the herbs that
perfume the hills of my town.

Could I then have listened more carefully
and heard the poetry of the master?
Thrilled by beauty, seeing God's wonders
in the transparent pink of the frail cyclamen.
Holding to the rock, shielded by a heart-shaped leaf,
Could I have looked more carefully
and perhaps have seen him there?

No. But I saw the town, huddled down.
I know its tempo and its throb,
slow but proud – inward-looking and not very holy.
I know the gossip, the pettiness, like every provincial town.
The poor, the sick, the haughty and the crafty,
and many a good heart, seen only by God.

O moon of my childhood, sitting bright, round, on the
   hill-top,
Did you also watch him
As he drank the beauty all around
And experienced a communion that transformed all around?
A light would shine,
A revelation
What reflection of eternity.

He rises and descends
to sup with Joseph and Mary.
Had he seen beyond the pink and blue of the horizon
A cross that loomed in the hazy beyond?

How did things go in the carpentry shop the next day?
Peasants came to order ploughs.
What talk took place between him and them?
Was it of harvests and of sheaves of corn?
What men came to order for doors,
tables and divans
where they would sup and recline?

Did anyone come to order for a cross?
For two pieces of wood?
How easy to make!
A shaft of light rested on the carpenter's face
from the slanted window with the iron bars.
It revealed his surprise, his innocence, his concern.
'What do you want this for?'

'For a Roman soldier who ordered it sir.'
'No, no, my friend.
Man must live
and not be crucified.'
Had a shudder gone through the master's body?
'Crosses! What crosses?
No. No crosses should be allowed.'
Next day the carpenter went to pray.
His theme was fixed, his revelation clear.

'I've come to bring sight to the blind,
hearing to the deaf,
freedom to those in prison,
and to preach the acceptable year of God.'

Three years passed
and where are the happy days of youth
and of illumination on the hill-top,
of Nazareth and the lilies of the field?

On Calvary stand three crosses,
not one.
Crosses, what crosses?
What do men want them for?
For judgement, for revenge!

'But I came to give you love.'

Could the master have remembered then
The carpentry, the shadow of the shaft of light,
that two poles are needed to make a cross?

The acceptable years? Are they gone?
The healing, the preaching and the fun?

What darkness in its grip holds the earth?
What grim evil power sways the land?
'Eli, Eli, Lama Shabactani.'

A ray of light shines,
the lilies of the field dance.
Eternity, Love.
'God I give myself,
I love you God, and all my fellow-men . . .
the Roman soldiers, my mother, John,
Mary, Peter . . .
Caiphas, Ananias and all the rest . . .
and Simon of Cyrene who carried my cross
. . . for this is your kingdom . . . '

Najwa Farah[11]

The carefree journey became the pilgrimage, and then became
the destination where the sole hope was in the giver of the
journey, the author of the pilgrimage, the mystery which we call
God. And it is on the mountain in many religious traditions
that God is encountered in awe, wonder and challenge, and it
is to the spiritual image of the mountain that we now turn.

NOTES

1. S. Kopp, *If You Meet the Buddha on the Road, Kill Him!* (Sheldon Press, London, 1994).
2. A. Bennett, *Writing Home* (Faber and Faber, London, 1994).
3. Brihadaranyaka Upanishad, *The Upanishads*, trans. Juan Mascaro (Penguin Classics, London, 1965).
4. N. Mandela, *Long Walk to Freedom* (Little, Brown and Company, London, 1994).
5. L. Tolstoy, *War and Peace* (Penguin Classics, Harmondsworth, 1982).
6. *Murder in the Cathedral*, in *The Complete Plays of T. S. Eliot* (Faber and Faber, London, 1964).
7. *Palestinian Pain and Promise* (Christians Aware, Leicester, 1992).
8. *Ibid.*

9. H. Hesse, *The Journey to the East* (Granada Publishing, London, 1972).

10. J. R. R. Tolkien, *The Lord of the Rings* (George Allen and Unwin, London, 1954).

11. *Palestinian Pain and Promise* (Christians Aware, Leicester, 1992).

CHAPTER TWO

Sacred Mountain

THE SACRED mountain as the meeting-place with God or the gods is a theme as old as time. Not surprisingly, when people inhabited a three-storey universe the gods were thought to dwell above the clouds, and mountains whose tops touched the clouds were therefore both awesome and holy places. In Greece, Mount Olympus was the home of the gods, who from time to time had fun altering the destinies of men and women. In such an unpredictable world how else could the changes and chances of life be explained? Mount Fuji to the Shinto practitioner of Japan, or Mount Kenya to the Gikuyu people were likewise places of holiness and awe, for there dwelt the gods.

We can get a notion of this amalgam of emotions regarding sacred mountains in the Biblical references to Mount Sinai. The awesomeness of the mountain was emphasized. No ordinary human being was to approach the mountain, and if any animals strayed onto it they were to be stoned to death. Moses alone climbed the mountain and even he did so with fear and trepidation because there was always the danger that the holiness of God would dazzle and consume a mere mortal. So Moses covered his face with a cloth to shield him from the direct sight of God, and even then his face glowed when he returned down the mountain so that the people had to turn away.

When the people of Israel eventually entered their promised land they created a sacred mountain in their very midst – the hill of Mount Zion, Jerusalem. Here Solomon built his temple, with its fringes for all peoples, its outer courts for Jewish men, its inner sanctuary where priests alone could go, and the holy of holies, entered only by the high priest. The temple, like a mountain, became the focus of the meeting-place with the holy God who determined destinies and who could bless or consume. But through their history around this sacred mountain the prophets and scholars tried to discern a pattern of God's providence which did not merely depend upon his capriciousness, like that of the gods on Olympus, but stemmed from righteousness and obedience. So morality and holiness began to be linked.

St Matthew's Gospel places the start of Jesus's public ministry very firmly on the mountain. For three chapters, starting with the 'Beatitudes', he teaches his disciples the morality which is to be expected of those called to be the holy people of God. More, he teaches the way in which God is to be approached in prayer. The 'Lord's Prayer' is at the heart of this 'mountain teaching' (Matt 6.9). It is clear that Matthew is seeing Jesus of Nazareth as the fulfilment of 'the Law and the Prophets', and just as Moses brought the old law and commandments to the people of Israel on Mount Sinai, made holy by the presence of God, so Jesus brings the new law and the new commandments of love and grace in his sermon on the mountain equally made holy by the presence of God.

In the same gospel we see this connection between morality, holiness, and the fulfilment of biblical promises in the story of the Transfiguration (Matt 17.2). Peter, James and John go up the mountain with Jesus and there they have a vision of him meeting with the great religious founders of their people and faith, Moses and Elijah. They are dazzled by the light of God's glory, and they hear the voice from God, 'This is my beloved Son . . . ' Their response is to stay with their peak experience but Jesus leads them down the mountain back to the everyday world of suffering and confusion, and immediately they are faced with the challenge of difficult healings and demands.

Of course we no longer live in a three-storey universe, and therefore do not see climbing a mountain as moving towards the glory of God, but the beauty, power and capriciousness of nature still draws many people to the challenge of climbing mountains. We have been fortunate over the years in being able to climb a number of mountains in Britain and overseas, including Mount Kenya, a mountain held in great awe by the Gikuyu people. We climbed with Gikuyu Christians whose ancestors had thought that God, Ngai, dwelt on the mountain; their own climb was something more than a pleasant outing. It was a serious journey, made so by the grandeur of the surroundings and the faith conversations of the climbers.

It seems to us that the methods mountaineers have developed for success and survival have echoes of the spiritual disciplines to be found in focused religious communities and people of faith. We would now like to examine the argument that poverty, chastity, and obedience are the basic principles of secular or spiritual mountaineering.

First let us consider poverty. Climbing can be exhilarating as well as breathtaking, with mind and body all in tune. But it can be terrifying. Perhaps you have been following what seemed to be a safe and secure fissure up the mountain-side. Maybe you have been entranced by the interest of the climb or the beauty of the scenery and then suddenly you have turned a corner and realized that you are on an exposed face and in danger. Your knees have turned to jelly, and you have done the natural thing and clung tight to the one thing that seemed secure – the rock face.

The problem is that you cannot climb whilst you are clinging tight. You may feel safe, but eventually as you cling you will die of exposure. Foolish though it may seem to the quivering legs, the only way to proceed is to push away from the face so that you have the balance to continue. If you watch skilful rock climbers at work, you will see that they are just touching the rock with fingers and toes and are moving up the face, balanced as though the empty air itself is carrying them.

The style of poverty is the style of living exposed before God and God's world. It is the style of pushing away from all idols which might give us a false sense of security but which will ultimately destroy us because they prevent us moving on in our journey to God. To proceed we must allow ourselves to be carried by God, even though that reality of God can sometimes feel less like a friend, and more like emptiness.

Jesus in his Sermon on the Mount points to the poor, the sorrowful, the meek and those mourning as being those who are blessed. Luke and Matthew in their gospels put different emphases upon whether Jesus was meaning the materially or the spiritually poor, but the point is surely the same. Poor people, whatever their poverty, are not blessed simply and automatically because they are poor. They are richly blessed, however, if through their poverty they know their need, their dependence upon God. The challenge, and it is a challenge to every person in one way or another, lies in being able to face up to poverty, loss, or distress and not to cling to false security by seeking palliatives.

People have many reasons to cling today, for the world is ever-changing and it is easy to feel exposed and insecure. It is easy for people, especially in the West, to live life in a taken-for-granted way, and this may continue for years. We may enjoy good times and cope with the difficulties calmly and efficiently, when suddenly the world shakes. In the family the children are growing up and having problems at school, or they have grown up and are having troubles with their jobs or housing or marriage. A friend of a friend dies of Aids. At work old jobs or ways of working disappear, new skills have to be learned or early retirement is firmly suggested. It sometimes feels as though we are living over an abyss of uncertainty and we would be less than human if we did not cling to anything which offers security. We cling to our favourite goods. We cling to our work and status, we cling to our family or friends, we cling to our religion.

The nearest idols to cling to when life denies us love and satisfaction are our possessions. They are always there to give us pseudo-security. When faced with an abyss without and within we need love and confidence but we will settle for a familiar room, or a flower garden, or a train in the attic, or a favourite TV programme, or another glass of wine, or a box of chocolates. But instant comfort is quite inadequate to fill the gaping hole at the centre of our spirit.

'You fool' says Jesus in Luke's story of the rich husbandman who, having worked hard and gained modest possessions, thought that he would put his feet up and take it easy. 'You fool, this night your soul will be required of you.' We must learn then to possess our possessions without being possessed by them. To handle them with a light touch and be prepared to move on.

Alexander Solzhenitsyn illustrates this so well in his novel, *The First Circle*.[1] He describes the life of Stalin, the most powerful man in the world, whose world had shrunk to one tiny room in the Kremlin, the only place where he could feel almost safe. He writes thus:

He felt that every one of his ministers was trying to hoodwink him. How could he possibly trust them? He had no choice but to work at nights. He was an old man without friends. Nobody loved him; he believed in nothing and he wanted nothing. Helpless fear overcame him as he sensed the dwindling memory, the failing mind. Loneliness crept over him, life paralysis. Death had already laid its hand upon him, but he would not believe it.

Some twenty pages later we are introduced to a prisoner in one of Stalin's labour camps.

Day was breaking. A thick rich hoar-frost feathered the posts of the fences, the score of intertwined strands, the thousand stars of the barbed wire, the sloping roof of the watchtower and the tall grass in the wilderness outside the compound. Clear-eyed Dmitry Sologdin gazed at the miracle and rejoiced in it. He wore a camp jacket over his blue denims, his head was bare, his hair showing the first streaks of grey. He was a slave, he had no rights. He had served twelve years but the end of his punishment was not in sight. His wife had wasted her youth waiting for him. Now, out of fear of losing her job, as she had lost so many others, she had lied to her employers, telling them she had no husband and had stopped writing.

All he owned was a pair of quilted trousers, stored away in expectation of worse times to come. He was paid thirty roubles a month, and not even that in cash. His hours in the fresh air were fixed and rationed by the prison authorities. But his soul was at peace. His eyes had the brightness of youth. Chest bared to the frost, he breathed deeply, as though inhaling the fullness of life, and faced the day with anticipation.

There it is in a nutshell. Don't cling. The man who owned everything and could literally move mountains and did, was still not able to find a secure hold on a life which was slipping away. The man who owned nothing, but who knew the abyss intimately as a close companion, was borne up and sustained by the wings of reality.

Yet pushing away from our possessions is often easier than pushing free from another convenient handhold, the idol called work and the meaning or status that it gives us. We human beings need admiration and praise as we need oxygen and if we cannot come by it naturally and freely in relationships of love and friendship, then we will snatch at it by power or authority or by finding self-dignity through the dignity of our role.

In the film of *One Flew Over the Cuckoo's Nest*[2] there was one brilliant scene which showed the patients breaking out from the mental hospital and stealing a fishing-boat. As they steered it out of the harbour, the harbour-master asked them who they were. They answered that they were a group of consultant psychiatrists on holiday. And all of a sudden they looked like doctors, and acted like doctors, and they received the honour due to doctors. Power and authority are given to the professional role, and those inhabiting the role can soon come to feel that respect is theirs by right.

But status and dignity apart, what of the work itself? Making an idol of our work can ultimately lead to two different stances. They are characterized for us in another novel by Solzhenitsyn, this time *Cancer Ward*,[3] in which he describes a visit to a zoo in a provincial Russian town. Just inside the entrance lie the empires of two very different kinds of animal. The one is a mountain goat, standing like a statue on the top of the rocks, still and immobile. The other is a squirrel inside a small wheel which is going faster and faster.

The visitor wants to shout, 'Stop, it's in vain', because otherwise it looks as though there is only one way out for the squirrel – death. We see both styles of activity in the workplace, home and church today, and in ourselves. We see the immobile goat, immobile because he is presiding over an empire from which everyone has departed and he doesn't know what to do next, or the frantic squirrel beavering away faster and faster, never finding the time to ask himself, 'How does this particular activity help me, my community, or my church – how does it relate to the Kingdom of God?'

Yet another idol to which even nations and national leaders are tempted to cling is the idol of wish-dreaming. Recently on a humanitarian visit to Iraq to see the effects of UN economic sanctions upon ordinary Iraqi people, we visited the site of the ancient city of Babylon. The guidebook states that nothing was left of the city except a marble lion. Not so. Saddam Hussein's regime has rebuilt Babylon – city walls, the temple, the palace, the ceremonial processional avenue – everything. And there at the entrance is a mural of King Nebuchadnezzar greeting Saddam Hussein. The message is clear – a new Nebuchadnezzar who will rebuild the great Babylonian empire is here. When present conditions are harsh, disappointing or challenging, it is tempting for any people or leader to cling to past glories or to future dreams and visions.

But the final idol to which we cling is perhaps the most persuasive, and it is the idol of certainty itself. In changing times in world and church, what can we be certain of that is unchanging, what ledge can we stand upon that is secure? Some people claim to have found the answer in an infallible institution, the community called Church. They see its traditional dogmatic claims and practices as having stood the test of time and culture. To the outsider the Church looks like the usual variety of messy human beings, quarrelsome, passionate, deluded, brave, frightened. To the believer, of course, this messy collection of human beings is the mystical body of Christ, through whose sacraments Jesus Christ, risen, ascended, glorified, is made present in a fallen world. The danger is that this latter visionary understanding of the Church through the eye and experience of faith becomes so dominating that the believer forgets that it is represented through ordinary human beings who can err, sometimes seriously. It is unwise to look for absolute certainty in any church.

Other people claim to have found certainty, not in an infallible institution but, if they are Christians, in an infallible collection of writings – the Bible. Again, from the outside the Bible is seen as just another collection of human experiences and ideas, subject to the normal disciplines of literary criticism, showing the mistakes, inconsistencies, touches of brilliance, pathos, and mundanity which you would expect to find in any compilation of writings coming from a variety of authors from different times and cultures. From the outside, then, the Bible is seen as a brilliant literary human creation.

From inside the community of faith the Bible is more than a collection of human writings: it is mysteriously God's word to God's world through which the Word made flesh, Jesus Christ, is preached afresh in time and space. Even with the insight of faith, however, it is unwise to see infallibility in every word or sentence. The Bible was written by many hands over many years and in many contexts, and some writers were more inspired than others. It is a unique spiritual treasure, but Christians do not worship a book, however inspired, they worship a godly person – Jesus the Christ.

We yield to none our love of the Church or of the Bible. But once we make an idol of either, they no longer carry the power of the living Christ, but become mere convenient handholds in our lust for certainty. The Church and Bible are fingers pointing to the reality of the living Christ. Their very purpose is to point beyond themselves to the God whom now we can only see through a glass darkly but whom, the apostle Paul promises us, we shall see face to face. And the reality of God has been glimpsed by the world in the pain-filled face of Jesus Christ.

But that takes us to the next discipline of spiritual and secular mountaineering, chastity. If poverty is the style of intentional detachment from all seemingly secure idols, chastity is willing one thing and pouring one's whole self into it. It is the drive which keeps rock climbers moving up the face with an economy of effort, with no squandered energy, their eyes on the way ahead.

Jesus in the Sermon on the Mount speaks of those who are blessed because they do what God requires, the merciful, the pure in heart, those who work for peace. These are the people of chastity who do not swerve from what is right and focus everything in pursuing it. In the traditional religious community, chastity shows itself in celibacy, but the celibacy is for this very purpose, to release the monk or nun from other human ties and responsibilities so as to will one thing with heart and mind and soul. There are many focused people around and they can give us examples of this sort of chastity. An international athlete, by definition, is such a person. Gary Lineker is quite a hero in Leicester, his home town, and it was whilst playing for Leicester City that he first found footballing fame. He has recently retired from his remarkable playing career, having played for distinguished clubs in Britain, Italy and Japan, and having captained his country on innumerable occasions. It has been said of him that he is the kind of man that every mother would like as a son, polite, courteous, thoughtful, smart. He certainly is the kind of player that every football manager would want in his side – skilful, imaginative, supremely fit. But above all, throughout his playing career he has been a focused man, concentrating on the game in hand and bringing out the best in himself and his fellow-players. In his whole playing career he has never been sent off the field. He has not allowed anger or emotion to break into his concentration – a man of chastity – focused, disciplined, willing one thing.

Another such person of chastity is the poet striving to find exactly the right word and the right combination of words so that not only meaning is communicated but emotion and vision – so that the reader is addressed not only mind to mind, but heart to heart, soul to soul. D. H. Lawrence, both novelist and poet, once wrote about his art:

Thought, I love thought.
But not the jiggling and twisting of already existent ideas.
I despise that self-important game.
Thought is the welling up of unknown life into consciousness.
Thought is the testing of statements on the touchstone of the conscience,
Thought is gazing on to the face of life, and reading what can be read,
Thought is pondering over experience and coming to a conclusion.
Thought is not a trick, or an exercise, or a set of dodges.
Thought is a man in his wholeness, wholly attending.[4]

That is quite a good description of the work of a person of chastity – focused, disciplined, willing one thing.

Another is the scientist wrestling with unconnected facts; poring over obscure mathematical formulae; putting forward a new hypothesis with humility and hope; performing the experiment and then watching with wonder and awe as fact after fact falls into place and confirms the hope. Or they don't, and the hypothesis is set aside and the whole process is patiently begun again. A postcard from one scientist, Joule, to another, Maxwell, sent in the last century after a particular breakthrough had taken place, encapsulates the focused thrill of the scientific quest. It reads, 'There are very few people who have stood where you stand, and after a period of patient manual effort and mental toil have put their minds in exact accordance with things as they really are.' That is the calling of scientific chastity.

We recently had the privilege of sharing a meeting with Professor James Watson. It is now over forty years since, with Francis Crick, he unravelled the mystery of the DNA helix which has opened up a whole new understanding of life and disease. Since that discovery forty years ago Professor Watson has given his professional life to fighting the ravages of genetic disease and serving those crippled with such diseases and those who care for them. Although retired, he is still passionately concerned with the latest developments in his field and committed to their further success – another person of chastity – focused, disciplined, willing one thing.

Then there is the man or woman engaged in some great cause, going out to right a great wrong, however long the struggle, and however great the price. The struggle has been long and difficult for those fighting apartheid in South Africa, and it continues in a new way now that the battle for democracy has been won. That the battle to end apartheid has been successful is in no small measure due to the people, famous and unknown, who have gone on and on, determined to bring change, dignity and new life to all the people of South Africa. The atmosphere of forgiveness and work for reconciliation which surrounded the first democratic elections and the establishment of the demo- cratic government of the new South Africa was possible partly at least because the leaders of the movement for change were bravely single-minded, totally dedicated to their task even when it seemed a very long way away, and forgiving of those who had opposed them. Nelson Mandela spent twenty-seven years in prison, but during that time he never forgot why he was there, or the task still before him of destroying apartheid. He rigorously planned for the future, and he challenged any detail of prison life which reflected the apartheid system, such as his doggedly determined campaign for the African prisoners to wear long trousers instead of the shorts which were meant to indicate that they were boys and not men.[5]

Oliver Cromwell, when he was forming his New Model Army, said, 'Give me soldiers who know what they fight for and love what they know.' Cromwell, it seems, wanted soldiers of chastity – focused, disciplined, willing one thing, and loving the thing they willed. The first time that he used that New Model Army the result was spectacular. At the Battle of Naseby, whilst Prince Rupert's cavalry charged, broke through the Parliamentary lines and then rode on cheerfully to ransack their camp a few miles away, Cromwell's soldiers reformed and struck again and again, destroying the bulk of the army of the Prince. The New Model Army was an army of chastity, focused, disciplined, willing one thing.

The Bible tells the story of the religious tribal leader taking his people from the land of slavery to the land of freedom, and getting mighty little thanks from them, for from the harshness of the desert journey even slavery has its attractions. Back in Egypt at least they had security and certainty. So Moses goes up the sacred mountain to have a little grumble to God about the wretched people God has given him to lead and care for (Exod 32). And the great Jehovah listens and agrees. He says in effect, 'Yes, I know, Moses, they are a dreadful crowd, and while you are up here grumbling to me, they are back down there making another idol – it looks like a golden calf. We will wipe them out and start again with better material.' That, of course, brought Moses to his senses. 'Just a minute. These are my people. I have sweated blood taking them to the promised land, and to the promised land they will go. Nobody, but nobody, wipes them out.' A man of chastity, focused, disciplined, willing one thing.

We come across a woman of chastity in the gospel story of Martha and Mary (Luke 10.40). Martha, not surprisingly, was thrown into a turmoil when a crowd of friends descended upon the house for afternoon tea. We know the feeling. A thousand and one things need to be done; the children need taking to town; the telephone is ringing; there is a knock at the door and in comes the crowd. So Martha busies herself in an effective kind of way, putting on a good domestic show and then notices that something or rather someone is missing – Mary. The cheek of it, there is Mary sitting chatting to Jesus, whilst she, Martha, is doing all the work. 'Tell Mary to help', she asks Jesus. But life is more than children, dinners, letters and telephone calls. 'Martha, Martha,' responds Jesus, 'one thing is needful. Mary has chosen the good, and it will not be taken from her.' Mary is the archetypal woman of chastity, focused, disciplined, willing one thing. 'Mary has chosen the good and it will not be taken from her; no, not in a thousand lifetimes.'

Chastity, then, is willing one thing, and Christian chastity is not one style amongst others. It is at the very heart of Christian discipleship. It is willing the good of God – the good shown to the world through the life and death and glory of Jesus Christ. To will anything less than the good of God is to make one more thing an idol, however noble the cause. We are called to will the Kingdom of God and to point others to that Kingdom and to the King who is its heart and soul. The quality of the cause we will determines the quality of the soul we have on our hands. And when we are willing the Kingdom of God, we are the Kingdom of God. We participate now. The Kingdom has come.

The squirrel on its wheel was living a life of active stupidity – always busy, doing one thing after another, with none having any particular depth. The mountain goat, alone and aloof, had the style of lucid laziness, superior in his vision, with a cynical view of the world around, yet equally frustrated in giving life to that vision. Chastity stands between those common attitudes of active stupidity and lucid laziness. The man or woman of chastity, centred in God, sees through to the very heart of the situation on hand, and then acts with a minimum of fuss and bother.

The third golden rule of mountaineering is, 'No one climbs alone'. If you would get anywhere near the summit of a mountain then you must travel with people who know the peaks and seriously mean to go there. Knowing who you climb with, who you say 'yes' to, is of ultimate importance, because your life might be in their hands, and theirs in yours. Having dealt with the traditional religious styles of poverty and chastity, we would like to call this 'saying yes' the style of obedience.

The basic question of obedience is 'What in the last resort am I loyal to? Whom do I ultimately trust? To what, or to whom do I say "yes" unconditionally? What, and whom do I obey?' This is very much a religious question. Around the island of Shikoku in Japan there are eighty-eight temples associated with events in the life of a great Buddhist saint, Kobo Daishi. For centuries Japanese pilgrims have made the thousand-mile pilgrimage around the island visiting the temples. On their pilgrimage they carry a stout stick and wear a hatband upon which is written the words, 'Dogyo ninin' which means, 'We two together'. The 'we two' refers to the Daishi and the pilgrim. It is thought that the Daishi accompanies and supports the pilgrim on the long pilgrimage. The stout stick is seen as a symbol of the Daishi's presence and support, so much so that it is treated with great respect, sometimes even being bathed and put to bed at the end of each day's pilgrimage. Obedience to the spirit and presence of the Daishi lies at the heart of the pilgrimage.

The religious discipline of obedience equally lies at the heart of Islam, indeed the very word 'Islam' means 'submission' –

obedience to the holy God. The opening chapters of the Qu'ran, recited as prayer in the mosque, make the Muslim approach to God very clear.

> In the name of God, the Merciful, the Compassionate!
> Praise be to God, Lord of the Worlds, the Merciful,
>   the Compassionate,
> Master of the Day of Judgement.
> Thee alone we worship, Thee alone we ask for help.

The essential elements of Islam involve submission to God, recognition of Muhammad as the messenger of God, and belief in the Qu'ran as the Holy Book of God. The understanding of Islam is that the individual's relationship with God is determined by his or her relationship with fellow human beings. The formation of 'Ummah', community, is a prime duty of Muslims, and it may be community on local, national or global levels. The Muslim says 'Yes' unconditionally to members of this community and fights for justice and equality amongst them. Obedience to God and loyalty to the Muslim community are symbolized in the '*Hajj*', which, as we indicated in the previous chapter, is the pilgrimage which every Muslim is challenged to make once in his or her lifetime; a journey which reinforces the solidarity and unity of all Muslims, no matter who they are or where they have travelled from. The reciting of the Qu'ran in Arabic gives Muslims a day-by-day reminder that they are at one with Muslims everywhere in the world.

Christians also share with Muslims an understanding of the spiritual discipline of obedience. In the Beatitudes we are taught that those who are happy are those who do what God requires of them, even to the point of persecution. When we lived in Zambia we once drove miles down a difficult dirt road near the border with the Congo, to visit a certain spot in the bush. There was a simple engraved stone marking the place where Dag Hammarskjöld, the first Secretary-General of the United Nations, was killed when his plane crashed whilst he was engaged in peace negotiations during the Congo war. In *Markings*, his journal published after his death, he wrote this:

I don't know who or what put the question to me, I don't remember answering, but I did answer 'Yes' and from that hour I was certain that existence is meaningful, and my life in self-surrender has a goal.[6]

There was a man of obedience, saying 'Yes', and through so doing finding a meaningful life.

If any of us would climb a mountain then we have no choice but to say 'Yes' to others, for the person who climbs alone ultimately may not survive. But not everyone seriously intends to climb. We sometimes go on holiday to Switzerland, where, in the mountainous regions at least, everyone looks as though they are great mountaineers. People spend endless time in the cafés and hotels in the valleys, poring over maps and guide books, and planning the best routes up the mountain. The climbing-shops are full of folk examining and trying on the latest clothing and equipment – clothing gleaming with colour, equipment magical in complexity. Some people even go out onto the hills, taking part in endless training walks around the foothills and meadows and ending up for afternoon tea or beer in one of the picturesque bars which clutter the lower slopes. Yet others are waiting around for the perfect guide; they are always dissatisfied with the one who led them last year and do not intend to start this year until the right one comes along; and they have very clear ideas of what such a guide should look like in terms of appearance, qualifications and training.

All these ways of passing the time are very pleasant, restful, or invigorating, but they do not get anyone far up the mountain. The spiritual quest similarly consists of many and various women and men who are not all equally serious in their endeavour. Many pay lip-service, some start, many get bogged down in spiritual guidebooks and holy equipment, some put their hope in the right guide coming along.

Christian spirituality is not ultimately based upon method or mystery. It is not dependent upon the right words or the right books. It is based upon what God has done in history through the life, death and glory of Jesus Christ. Christians believe that he is the guide God has given and there is no point in waiting around for any other. Christian obedience consists of saying 'Yes' to that initiative of God, and walking with those who trust in its power and grace.

There are plenty of those who claim special revelations, secret knowledge, mystical methodology – authoritarian sects of all sorts abound. In the early Church some of these people were known as Gnostics, and Gnosticism permeated many faiths including Christianity. In the dialogue with the claims and culture of Gnosticism it became apparent that orthodox Christianity at heart was a straightforward saying 'Yes' to what God had already done through Jesus in history, responding in obedience to God's claim on our lives, and this is still the understanding of the mainline Christian churches today.

This does not mean that we will not have our moments of vision, but in the Bible vision is always associated with obedience. Moses, stunned by the burning bush, is immediately given a job to do, to confront Pharaoh with the challenge, 'Let my people go'. And in obedience to that task he caught further glimpses of the glory of God. The apostle Paul witnessed to the same reality to King Agrippa. He did not say, 'King Agrippa, I received a marvellously uplifting vision on the Damascus road. King Agrippa, believe this, and do that, and you too can see the wonder of God.' No, he said, 'King Agrippa, I was not disobedient to the heavenly vision.' The apostle in his obedience was only following the example of his Lord Jesus the Christ, who followed the way of his heavenly Father through life and death and life and glory (Acts 26.19).

The sacred mountain, then, teaches us helpful disciplines for lives which would relate closely to God. Poverty is striving to push away from all secure idols, and trusting in the fullness or emptiness of God to carry us. Chastity is disciplined and focused living, willing one thing, God's good, for ourselves and those whom we love and serve, for God's Church, for God's world. Obedience is having said 'Yes' to Jesus Christ and to one another, climbing with confidence and even delight, knowing that though we may travel across steep ravines and dark precipices, the glorious uplands of God's Kingdom lie before us.

Poverty, chastity and obedience are the style of the mountaineer, the style of spirituality at its best, and we end this chapter with a story from the Buddhist tradition which was retold in the West in *The Ronin*[7] and which powerfully summarizes these spiritual disciplines.

The story tells of a young prince who wanted to be a swordsman. The best tutors were hired to teach him swordsmanship, but they were naturally frightened at the possibility of hurting the prince and so they let the boy win make-believe fight after fight. The boy had, after a while, the sense to see that he was learning nothing and the tutors were dismissed. He finally heard of an old swordsman who had retired to a life of prayer and meditation in a clearing in the forest high up on a mountain. Despite the old man's protestations he was persuaded to take the boy on as a pupil. The boy exchanged the life of the palace for the more basic lifestyle of his tutor.

The boy was told that it was his job to keep the fire in the clearing going night and day. For a time he enjoyed doing this, but after a month he was bored and politely asked his tutor when his training was to begin. The old man looked sharply at him and told him that from now on, as well as keeping the fire going night and day, he would have to go down the hill to the river a dozen times a day, and bring back two buckets of water each time, so that he, his tutor, could have a bath each evening.

At the end of a year of this heavy work, the boy was worn out and he told himself that he'd made a big mistake. He vowed that by the light of the next full moon he would return home to the palace – but something happened before then which drove all thoughts of returning out of his mind. Something happened – and it hurt. As he was bringing one of the buckets up the hillside, he was felled by a blow. He looked up to see his tutor standing over him, holding a bamboo stick which had been obviously cut especially for that purpose. The boy scrambled for safety into the woods as blows rained down upon him.

From then on life was dangerous, for at any moment the boy might walk into an ambush. He learnt to be always alert. He learnt to distinguish the sound of an animal or bird from the footfall of his tutor. He became so sensitive that one afternoon he came upon his tutor waiting in ambush, but facing the other way. The boy crept silently away again, but the old man had seen, and that evening he presented the boy with his own stick. It was the proudest moment of the boy's life.

But the boy's anxiety did not end, for now, as well as keeping the fire going night and day, as well as having to bring innumerable buckets of water up the mountain, at any moment he had to engage in a furious fight with his tutor, a fight which he always lost – it wasn't a question of winning, it was simply a question of whether the fight could be kept going for a few minutes longer than the previous one, before his stick would be struck from his hands and the cruel stick of his tutor would crash down onto his shoulder once more.

But he was learning, and after a while his concern was not to hurt his tutor too much in the fights that he was increasingly winning. After five years he was the finest swordsman in the land, although he did not realize it. His tutor sent a message to the palace, and in a ceremony of great dignity, the prince was presented with a magnificent sword. It never again left his side. He never had to use it.

There was no cheap way of becoming a swordsman, and there is no cheap way of pursuing the spiritual path. The early tutors, for their own reasons, had denied the boy skill. It was only the loving, single-minded commitment of the old man, calling forth a similar commitment in the boy, which gave the boy his heart's desire, a costly skill, costly earned. Prince and tutor were men of poverty, chastity and obedience – pushing away from all security, focusing on the task in hand, obedient to their calling. Spiritual mountaineering is exciting and exhilarating, but it cannot be cheaply pursued. The keys to the climb are the disciplines of poverty, chastity and obedience and then no mountain is unclimbable, no life is unliveable, and no world is unsavable.

NOTES

1. A. Solzhenitsyn, *The First Circle* (Collins, London, 1969).
2. K. Kesey, *One Flew Over the Cuckoo's Nest* (Methuen, London, 1962).
3. A. Solzhenitsyn *Cancer Ward* (Penguin Books, Harmondsworth, 1971).
4. 'More Pansies', in *D. H. Lawrence – the Complete Poems* (Penguin Books, Harmondsworth, 1977).
5. N. Mandela, *Long Walk to Freedom* (Little, Brown, London, 1994).
6. D. Hammarskjöld, *Markings* (Faber and Faber, London, 1964).
7. W. D. Jennings, *The Ronin* (Charles E. Tuttle, Rutland, VT, 1968).

CHAPTER THREE

Sacred Land

HUMANKIND HAS occupied every continent on earth. It has been at home in the tropical rain forests, in the forest margins surrounded by crashing falls and stampeding zebra. It has shared the life of the vast plains, hunting and gathering beneath the ever-present sun. It has lived with grumbling volcanoes, and earth-splitting earthquakes. It has crossed icy passes and built villages clinging like eyries to mountain ledges. It has burrowed into the snow of the Arctic tundra and, with the polar bear and seal, survived six months of darkness annually. And now it has left the earth and made a home in a metal box spinning around the earth, and even set foot on the moon. And everywhere it has regarded the land as a sacred home – to be treated with respect and even awe; everywhere, that is, until the relatively recent experience of living in cities, cut off from immediate contact with the earth.

The detachment from the earth has been a gradual but continuous process. One image of this is a box. Men and women, in order to survive and prosper in a sometimes hostile world, have in effect gradually constructed a box of urbanization and domestication, shutting themselves off from the basic danger and wonder of existence. The first wall of the box was security. There is a Celtic prayer, 'Lord your sea is so large, and my boat is so small.' That has been the experience of most of humankind most of the time. To stand on an African plain surrounded by the vastness of the bush under the unrelenting power of the sun, with dangerous animals perhaps behind every tree, is to feel small, insignificant and vulnerable.

In that situation humankind built a wall of security: a cave or a hut surrounded by a thorn fence where some safety could be found. And then humankind, a species with weak bodies and large brains, began to form into wider tribal groups so as to hold its own amongst the bloody market-place of nature – the wall of community was constructed, enabling weak individuals to feel strong in defence, in hunting, and in organizing food growing and family nurture. Before long, with technology ever changing what was possible, new developments in metal working, new strains of grain and new building materials were seen. The gathered huts behind thorn fences became towns or cities behind stone walls, shutting out the danger and the wonder of nature.

And in those cities, not everyone had to do everything – specialization of work and roles appeared together with hierarchies in society. For many, there was time left over after the essential work had been done. It was no longer necessary to work every minute of daylight and sleep exhausted through the hours of darkness in order to survive. There was time to spare; there was time for a culture to blossom and grow; for basic dance and music to become more sophisticated; for oral stories, related previously by the elders around the fire at night, to be written and recorded and stored on stone and parchment; for social customs to be codified into laws; and for systems of judgement and appeal to be developed so that everyone felt that they had a stake in society.

The great civilizations often proceeded down this path of increasing urbanization, but they paid a price for doing so. In the secure box which they had created there was indeed some security, predictability, stability and even, for the fortunate, job satisfaction – but what tended to be shut out was the awe, wonder and excitement of a more primitive way of life. But it is not inevitable that awe, wonder and the zest for adventure should be shut out from urban society. A rich, developing culture should be ever opening the human spirit to new vistas, and religion should be the window in the wall of civilization which reminds humankind of its roots and of its ultimate destiny, feeds its life with the grace and power of the creator spirit behind nature, and drives the arrow of the civilizing adventure. But for many Western people in recent decades religion no longer acts as that open window to a more awesome existence. At best it has became merely a beautiful part of the wall, just as a stained-glass window, however beautiful, blocks out the views to the outside. At worst religion has become a small domesticated private box or series of boxes for people who like that kind of activity.

But there is also a new and unpredictable spirit around – associated with the general title of 'New Age' – which is seeking to return to, or rediscover, the symbiotic link between humankind and nature. It further seeks a more primitive sense of the sacredness of the land, of the earth. It is this sacred land which we want to explore in this chapter, by revisiting some of the civilizations which have not totally sold out to urbanization, and by beginning to discern what wisdoms there are for New Age spiritual travellers who wish to revisit their roots.

A watershed moment occurred with the landing on the moon in the late 1960s. One of the Apollo team, Bill Anders, on seeing the earth for the first time from the perspective of space, said, 'We've come all this way to explore the moon, and the most important thing is that we've discovered the earth.'

His perception was shared by millions of those who saw the same picture. There were no national boundaries – just an intermingling of land and sea enfolded by swirling cloud – a marble of colour, light and life, floating in the immensity of dark space. Many people both felt protective of our beautiful globe and had a new awareness of its vulnerability; religious feelings of awe, wonder, and fear were suddenly the common currency.

It is perhaps ironic that one consequence of this ultra-scientific project, probably not to be repeated in our lifetime, was a strengthening of the New Age movement which takes its title from the unscientific belief of astrology. For the phrase 'New Age' refers to the shift from the 'Age of Pisces', which corresponds roughly to the Christian Era, to the 'Age of Aquarius', which is apparently to dawn some time between now and 2062. We are, of course, also approaching the end of the millenium and this gives an added impetus to this sense of a dawning new age.

The New Age movement is a confusing mix of ecology, spirituality, alternative lifestyles, and irrationality. Its very attraction for many people is the way in which there are no set dogmas, no religious or scientific creeds, no traditions or disciplines to be studied or mastered. In this way it differs substantially from traditional societies around the globe which otherwise share its respect for nature and its openness to the world of ancestors and spirits.

Let us examine examples from traditional societies in a little more detail. We have had some firsthand experience of African and Aborigine cultures. If the preoccupation of the Western world, certainly since the Enlightenment, has been rationality and the quest for meaning and understanding within the social development of the nation-state, with a religion, Christianity, whose liturgy is ordered and whose wisdom is communicated through the development of the word, then the preoccupation of traditional African society has been with vitality, and the quest for harmony and rhythm within the social organization of the tribe, and a religion whose life is a total immersion within the spirit world, focused by the shaman whose charisma brings the spirits under control.

The land is home, food, protection, danger and the mask of the spirit world. Life is a constant struggle for the use of land – hunting, gathering, or slash-and-burning to provide fertile land for growing food. The land is to be approached with humility, for so much is not under control. 'To find one honey comb is good fortune. To find two is wonderful. To find three is witchcraft!' The seed must be planted before the rains. Plant too soon and the new shoots grow and wither before the rains arrive, plant too late and there is not enough time for the crop to ripen. It is not only a matter of judgement, it is a matter of being on good terms with the spirit world.

The notion of the spirit world controls social life, agriculture, health and education. Wisdom is passed down from generation to generation through the tribal stories of the elders and the initiation ceremonies of young women and warriors. The tribal stories not only remind the tribal members of 'who they are and where they come from', they also relate how the ancestor brought the tribe to their particular piece of land – they are the guarantee that the tribe has a right to be there. There is a lengthy example of tribal stories in the early books of the Old Testament – not only the story of their creation and call, but the story of how the people of Israel came to their 'promised land' and the covenant which they had made with God.

What are the components of traditional African life and spirit? Behind the world is a universal creative force and primal power which is never seen. There are secondary powers in charge of the earth, giving nature its vitality. Such powers are behind mountains, lakes, rivers, forests, and even individual trees. Again these powerful spirits are hidden behind the mask of nature – the very mountains, trees, sun and sky which they control.

The individual man or woman stands before such spirit power hidden by the mask of nature and feels alone, vulnerable and fragile. Yet the individual is not alone – he or she always stands with the tribe. And the living members of the tribe are not alone because behind them are the spirits of the ancestors who protect and encourage the living, provided the spirits are honoured, their shrines cared for, and their memories respected. Even so there is an imbalance – the primal powers stand behind nature's mask, yet the individual and the tribe have no such protection. In such an imbalance of power, energy and vitality are drained away and people are left like dry husks, unable to fight, hunt or love.

So, to restore the balance, the tribe produces its own masks behind which it stands. These take various and exotic forms depending upon the 'face' which the tribe wishes to show to the spirit world. The tribe and its members, with the spirits of the ancestors at their shoulders, stand behind the tribal masks and face the primal spirits behind their mask of nature. But this is a static position – a spiritual stalemate. For new life and energy to be produced there must be rhythm. And here we come to the heart of African traditional spirituality. If the heart of Christian spirituality lies in the words, 'In the beginning was the word', then the heart of African spirituality might be in the words, 'In the beginning was the beat' – the beat of the universe, the pulse of life.

And so the tribe, in ritual song and dance carried by the incessant beat of the drum, tunes into the beat of the universe. In this way its energy and power are preserved, sustained and enhanced. But the ritual is more powerful than this, for not only does the tribe tune in to the beat of the universe, it gradually, as the tempo increases, imposes its own beat upon the beat of the primal powers. It makes the spirits work for its particular pressing need, whether this be hunting, war, initiation or sex. The ceremonies are direct and vivid, but above all they are carried by charismatic drumming which is meant, literally, to be 'out of this world'. Beauty, laughter, sorrow, exhaustion take over in a kind of corporate catharsis which heals and renews.

There are social roles within this integrated world. Social power is exercised by the tribal elders symbolized by the tribal chief. When a decision has to be made the elders will gather under the 'palaver tree' and talk for days until the chief discerns that a consensus is emerging. He will then express his decision. This is no Western-type democracy but it is a foolish chief whose decision is often at odds with the consensus of the elders. The shaman is the ritual leader who knows the appropriate masks, discerns when the time is right for the rituals and then leads and guides the dance. The shaman is the living doorway into the spirit world. He or she can be dangerous, for evil spirits may flow through the shaman to the enemy, but equally the shaman has the power to kill soul sickness, to speak the word which counteracts curses, and give people permission to live their lives in peace.

What then might be the gifts of such a society to a 'New Age People' wishing to learn from traditional ways and wisdoms? Every person is cared for by every person – nobody is disconnected from the common life and nobody is disconnected from the land and from the cosmos. Success in the life of people automatically links to success in the life of the cosmos. The battle of life, the struggle between life and death, is fought by people within the context of their land, the natural elements, cosmic forces, and living and dead people. The Jesuit artist and writer, Engelbert Mveng from the Cameroun,[1] has suggested that the individual is not a person in the African meaning of the word, but simply an outline which must be filled in by integration with the cosmos, the land and society. Society includes the dead ancestors who are buried on the community lands. In many tribes they are buried next to the homes of their extended families. Africans visiting Britain for the first time are sometimes surprised when they see graveyards for the dead, far away from their families. Western people do not always appreciate how calamitous it is when African people have to leave their lands, for whatever reason. Leaving the land is leaving all rootedness behind with the ancestors. It is a great tragedy. Ngugi Wa Thiongo has often written about people in Kenya being driven off their lands at the time of colonization, and preferring to stay and work for the colonizer rather than become uprooted and lost.[2] In *Matigari*,[3] first published in Gikuyu, Ngugi tells of a man who emerges from the mountains after independence and searches for his family and lands. The search becomes a battle when he finds the family still dispossessed of its lands, and he is in his turn challenged by those who see him as a trouble-maker. When Matigari returns to the lands of his ancestors he tells those living in the house and running the surrounding tea plantation that he was there from the very beginning and has seen all the changes which have taken place. His own hands were those which built the plantation, and the house is his house.

Matigari is told that he is fettered to his clan and to his family and that he does not understand the freedom of the individual. This is quite true, he does not understand it, for he is a traditional African, not an isolated individual. His sense of community goes back to those who were there at the beginning, to the land and to the whole cosmos. He has a unified understanding, he is a whole person and his religion binds everything together so that it makes sense. Every ceremony, every dance, every piece of music and every work of art is a linking up of all that is, including the world of the spirits.

The holistic African understanding and approach to life, the land and the cosmos is similar to the Old Testament understanding, which is why the Old Testament has such an important place in the African churches. African Christians see no difference between the religious realm and the secular realm, for all relates to God. People see God as part of the rich tapestry of their world and the beyond, and they know their need of him in every minute of life, work and death. They pray in all situations and they understand their relationship to God as directly linked to what he may do for them. Their faith is dynamic, it is alive and vibrant and it liberates con-gregations for powerful community worship, including song and dance. Some of the churches originating in the West are trying to catch up with the independent churches in developing a holistic approach to faith, life and the beyond. One of the ways in which this is done is for some churches to allow traditional music and dancing within church services. Some new liturgies are being developed which link traditional culture with

Christian faith. The Anglican Church in Kenya has produced a new liturgy of Holy Communion which is both biblical and Kenyan.[4] One prayer is, 'Gracious Father, we heartily thank you for our faithful ancestors. We pray that we may walk in their footsteps and be fully united with them in your heavenly kingdom.' Other prayers are offered in thanksgiving for flocks, herds and fish, and for the fields to be fertile and the harvest good.

Christians in Africa are rediscovering what they have always known, that life has a rhythm and we are wise if we tune into the beat of the universe, resonate with it, stomp it out in liturgical life, and expect to be changed by it. Equally, all of us perhaps need to realize that we all look out onto a mysterious world through masks, and we are wise if we choose the masks that preserve spirit and do good.

The Spanish artist Pablo Picasso was greatly influenced by African masks. When he was living and painting in Paris he visited the Ethnographic Museum in the Louvre. What he saw there gave him a new inspiration and a change of direction in his own work. He said of the African masks and sculptures, 'Men have created those works for a sacred purpose, a magic purpose.' And he went on to say about his own work, 'Painting is not an aesthetic operation. It's a kind of magic, a way of seizing power by giving form to our terrors as well as to our desires.'

After seeing these African artefacts Picasso painted *Les Demoiselles d'Avignon 1907*, which was seen as 'incomprehensibly savage' even by his fellow-artists, but has later been seen as the seminal work of Cubism. It was painted at a time when science and philosophy were questioning conventional portrayals of reality, and were putting forward a more ambiguous and multi-faceted view of the world. It is significant that it was the basic and direct art of traditional Africa which gave Picasso the inspiration, through Cubism, to respond to this new world.

It is interesting to compare the African understanding and approach to life, the land and the cosmos with the similarly holistic understanding of Native Americans. When the settlers in 1854 wished to purchase a huge tract of Indian land and create in return a 'reservation', Chief Seattle replied:

How can you buy or sell the sky, the warmth of the land? If we do not own the freshness of the air and the sparkle of the water, how can you buy them? Every part of this earth is sacred to my people. This earth is precious to [God] and to harm the earth is to heap contempt on its creator.[5]

In 1911 the only surviving member of the small Yahi tribe was found in California. He was taken to live and work at the University of California Museum of Anthropology, where he spent the last five years of his life. It seems that he still managed to live a gentle and spirit-filled life but it is deeply ironic that the only place this impressive man could find a role in modern society was within a museum.[6]

The Bishop of Alaska, himself a Choctaw Indian, points out that America's tribal people shared with ancient Israel a deeply theological understanding of the intimate relationship between people, land, and nationhood. He suggests that, for Americans, their national 'Old Testament' is their native culture, and to understand it leads to a better understanding of themselves.[7]

Now what of the different, yet related, traditional culture of the Australian Aborigine? Could it be that Aborigine culture is humankind's 'Old Testament'? Bruce Chatwin's travel book *The Songlines*[8] has opened up the power of the aboriginal world to a global readership, and never has there been more interest in aboriginal culture and art. Australian rock paintings go back some eighteen thousand years but authentic aboriginal art is still being produced, and in many ways aboriginal culture is unique in that it is possible to have a dialogue in the here and now with traditions which have changed little in those eighteen thousand years. For Aborigines as for traditional Africans the visible world is steeped in the spirit realm.

As with traditional African religion, aboriginal religions are of great complexity and sophistication. 'Dreaming' is at the heart of the aboriginal world-view, but 'dreaming' in no way suggests an unreal or dream-like quality; on the contrary, to the Aborigine, it is of the essence of reality. Their understanding is that the primordial ancestor spirits shaped the land and gave to each aboriginal people their codes of conduct. Before creation time the earth existed as a flat featureless plain without the covering of grass or trees, without mountains or rivers to give distinguishing features. Yet dreaming beneath the surface were forms of life which would shape the land and society. These primeval creatures emerged and lived and fought and died. The

Aborigines look upon themselves as the direct descendants of these mythical creatures, linked to them and the land they shaped by story, ritual and art.

Spirits, it is thought, still inhabit the land, some harmless, some ill-disposed. There are also giant rainbow serpents who live in rivers and deep water-holes who will drown anyone foolish enough to drink their water without making the correct rituals. Other spirits are forever trying to suck the spirits of sick people from their bodies, and there is no understanding of death from natural causes. Death is a result of enemy magic, and complex rituals are constantly needed to prevent such calamity, or to identify the cause when it occurs.

There are also myths of major ancestral figures whose paths crossed tribal areas. Such myths give meaning to geographical features in the landscape and explain their form and also decree the rules of behaviour for harmonious living. Dreaming is not a past reality, therefore, it is something alive and active, the power of which is ever sustaining and invigorating all living things. This life-force permeates everything and is focused in religion and art, which both commemorate and enable people to tap into the spiritual power of life. An object of art, then, has more the nature of an icon – not something to be looked at or admired but a religious object to be used. Having said that, the religious reality behind such artefacts is not readily available to the casual observer. Indeed much of the spirit-wisdom which is being conveyed is jealously guarded not only from outsiders, but from others within the kinship group. Sacred secrets are preserved by not divulging a picture's meaning – knowledge is power in aboriginal society.

To Western eyes familiar with Jungian art-forms there is an immediate connection with the motifs – the circles, the snakes, the spirals, the maze-like paths. It is as though these pictures have tapped some deep source, not only within tribal history in a far-away country but within the souls of contemporary Western individuals. Of course many modern aboriginal paintings are no longer made for ceremonies but for the international art market. Nor are they merely produced for the profit of the individuals or art schools which produce them. They often carry a powerful message – 'This is my country' – the painting has become a political statement to a world which up until now has undervalued or even despised a proud people. Aboriginal art acts in so many ways as a bridge – between cultures; between colonialists and the dispossessed; between ancient and modern; between the ego and the self. A story is told of one aboriginal group of ancestors who set off in search of living water, and as they went they stopped from time to time and sang. But when they found the living water 'they went underground, and they are there today'. To touch aboriginal art is to risk taking that journey into the depths where perhaps living water is to be found.

With this background, what sense can we make of the 'New Age Movement' and some of its products? The movement finds a focus in a discontent with the existing way of life in Western society, and with associated thought and religion. It is concerned with creation and nature at both macro and micro levels – Amazonian rain forests and ecology centres in local schools. It is holistic, wanting to see the removal of boundaries not only between nations, religions and peoples, but within the individual, bringing mind, body and spirit together. Hence there is an interest in all varieties of fringe medicine and therapies. There is an anxiety about Western logical knowledge and particularly Western science, which it sees as bringing the earth to the edge of destruction. Thus there is an emphasis on the importance of the irrational, and the magical world of astral and mystical forces has a consequent appeal. Some of these themes obviously have connections with the religious world-systems of traditional Africa or the aboriginal world, but the significant difference is that those traditional systems are systems – coherent, self-sufficient and sustaining, with codes, myths, rituals and order. One feature of the New Age Movement is that it is a movement rather than a system, an eclectic gathering of people, ideas and methods both ancient and modern, with no coherent system or order. It is interesting, perhaps, to dip into as a bored individual but impossible to live by or to arrange a society around.

The New Age Movement is beginning to influence mainstream religion, however. Perhaps the clearest indication of this in Christian circles is Matthew Fox's 'creation-centred spirituality'.[9] Fox has been influenced by the beliefs and practices of the native American Indians who, as we have seen, have a similar shamanistic and earth-centred approach to that of traditional African and aboriginal cultures. He tries also to reclaim a tradition of creation-centred spirituality through Christian mystics such as Meister Eckhart, Julian of Norwich and St Irenaeus.

He argues that the Christian tradition has over-emphasized the fall/redemption tradition with its dualism, guilt and pessimism, with consequent implications for asceticism, power and patriarchy. He would want to emphasize 'original blessing' rather than 'original sin', an approach which would present creativity, optimism, sensuality and passion with aestheticism rather than asceticism, prophecy rather than power structures, and feminism rather than patriarchy. He details four paths: befriending creation; befriending the darkness; befriending creativity; and befriending the new creation. He sees Christ as the exemplar in following these paths which lead to self-emptying, letting go, sinking into nothingness, and realizing our own divinity as co-creators with God. He sees 'Mother Earth' crucified by patriarchy and fascist fundamentalism, a constantly sacrificed paschal lamb, but through 'Mother Cosmos' a deep mystical awakening will come – a resurrection story for our time.

This teaching, though attractive and exciting to many, has not surprisingly disturbed other practising Christians who feel that Fox, whilst being right in claiming that we have not stewarded the earth well and right in his accusation of an imbalance in the Western tradition, is wrong to polarize positions in this way, and perhaps wrong in his interpretation of scripture.[10]

Fox's notion of 'Mother Cosmos' providing a spiritual awakening has echoes in another significant development, this time in modern science – the 'Gaia Hypothesis'.[11] This is the theory of Dr James Lovelock that the earth's biosphere acts as a single living entity, self-regulating so as to maintain suitable conditions for its own survival. Humanity is an element in this biosphere, but a potentially dangerous element because it can act like a parasite which destroys the host. Perhaps by giving the hypothesis the name 'Gaia' (a Greek earth-goddess) Lovelock was encouraging an overlap with New Age thought, although he insists that this was not his intention. He has written, 'Gaia as a name, or a sign, has extended far beyond my intentions . . . I watch it filling fast, and mostly with rubbish, like an empty skip left on a London street.'[12]

Be that as it may, Gaia has formed a significant bridge between environmentalists who would like to see a spiritual dimension behind their concerns and New Age 'mystics and misfits' who like to see a little scientific grit in their mystical and magical soup. It is an interesting conjunction of images and disciplines. In the words of Lovelock, it is defined as a 'complex unity involving the Earth's biosphere, atmosphere, ocean and soil; the totality constituting a feedback or cybernetic system which seeks an optimal physical and chemical environment for life on this planet' – words which should satisfy the most hard-nosed scientist or Greenpeace activist; and yet Gaia by its very name carries the concept of 'Mother Earth', an image to be found within religion, art and literature. Perhaps because of this, Gaia has given rise to an industry of books, and the *Gaia* magazine, containing a fascinating mixture of science, environmental politics and spirituality, was launched in 1990.

It seems that there are many people in the Western world who find traditional forms of Christianity uninspiring and unhelpful for their condition. Perhaps they even find it unspiritual. They are thoroughly 'modern' in their lifestyles and world-views and yet have a deep sense of unsatisfied spiritual longings, and they have a profound concern for the life of the planet and future generations. Some churches have attempted to respond to these interests, longings and concerns. In London, St James's Church, Piccadilly, is known for its 'New Age' seminars, dances, liturgies and meditations, but there are ways in which 'Gaia issues' are permeating the Church in less dramatic forms. We recently visited St John's Episcopal Cathedral in New York. It is a vast cavern, built on Gothic lines. Every chapel was occupied by a school group and was dedicated to some aspect of the world's ecology – rain forests, whales, fish, giant pandas, urban farms – all were there in profusion and the children were being led on a fascinating journey of ecological exploration within the spiritual setting of a giant cathedral.

Of course the great Gothic cathedrals of Western Europe have always provided a kind of spiritual forest for worshippers and visitors. In the half-light filtering in through stained-glass windows the pillars are like stone tree trunks whilst the arches form fingers which intermingle and interlock like the branches in a forest. The carved corbels watch and peep and wink like

elves and goblins. We are not too far away from the primitive
magical world of ancient humanity. And yet this ancient magical
and perhaps spiritual input is presented in a controlled and even
'safe' way so that urban women and men, living in their secure
though dull boxes, can be reminded of their deeper selves, without the images and powers within emerging in an uncontrolled
and frightening way and causing breakdown or neurosis. And
these primitive, ancient and ambiguous art-forms form the shell
of a building within which Christian prayer, ritual and teaching
are being offered – as though the primitive spiritual world has
been 'baptized' and enlightened by the religion which finds its
meaning and inspiration in Jesus Christ, an ambiguous figure
pointing both to Jesus of Nazareth, the charismatic Galilean
teacher and healer, and Jesus the Cosmic Christ, ruling the
universe beyond time and space.

The practice of 'baptizing' places of pagan worship for use as
churches was recommended by Pope Gregory to Augustine
when he prepared for the mission to England. Gregory argued,
'In this way, we hope that the people, seeing that its temples are
not destroyed, may abandon idolatry and resort to these places
as before, and may come to know and adore the true God.'[13]
Still today a number of ancient English parish churches stand
on the sites of even more ancient holy places. Sometimes old
traditions were reinterpreted. One example of this is the way
that the pre-Christian legend of Glastonbury Tor as the place
of burial of a magic cauldron of plenty was replaced by the
story of Joseph of Arimathaea's burial of the Holy Grail. The
attempt was made then to ensure that the numinous power
associated with certain places, felt to be spirit-filled, was
channelled through the liturgies of the Christian faith which
would give new shape to local devotion and link it with the
eternal purposes of God as revealed in Jesus Christ.

A Christian spirituality from those times which is being redis-
covered and reinvigorated today, perhaps because it contains
many of the elements which we have been examining here –
respect for nature, deep spirituality, unhierarchical organization
and simple lifestyles – is the spirit of Celtic Christianity. In the
fourth century Celtic saints put out to sea in small boats, not
knowing where wind or wave would take them. And when they
landed they preached the gospel – so that hermitages, and then

monasteries, were established around the coasts of northern
Britain and Europe, and from these beach-heads missionaries
penetrated into the heart of the country. Their way was to
'baptize' what they found for Christ. They were prepared for
the Christian message to be grafted on to the stem of the local
religions. Their belief was that God is not in us, but we are in
God. Their spirituality saw life as an unbroken whole. This
world and the next overlapped. They were 'God-intoxicated'
people with a sense of the real presence of God in places and
people. Celtic Christianity flourished in the sixth century and,
although eventually overshadowed by the organization and
structure of Rome, it could be that its time has come again as
the millennium approaches, and we rediscover our unity with
nature and seek for a spirituality which will feed our souls and
yet be authentically Christian.

Here is a flavour of Celtic writing, traditionally thought to
have been written by a prince called Amerigin and to be the
earliest poem surviving in Ireland:

> I am the wind which breathes upon the sea.
> I am the wave of the ocean.
> I am the murmur of the billows.
> I am the vulture upon the rocks.
> I am the beam of the sun.
> I am the fairest of the plants.
> I am the wild boar in valour.
> I am the salmon in the water.
> I am a lake in the plain.
> I am a word of knowledge.
> I am the point of the lance in battle.
> I am the God who created the fire in the head.[14]

But what of the 'pain in the heart'? We turn next to the subject
of 'sacred suffering'.

NOTES

1. T. Witvliet, *A Place in the Sun* (SCM Press, London, 1985).
2. J. Ngugi, *A Grain of Wheat* (Heinemann, London, 1967).
3. J. Ngugi, *Matigari* (Heinemann, London, 1987).
4. *A Modern Service of Holy Communion* (CPK, Uzima Press, Kenya, 1989).
5. *Areopagus*, Vol. 4, No. 2, Lent 1991.

6. T. Kroeber, *Ishi in Two Worlds* (University of California Press, Berkeley, 1976).
7. M. Perry, *Gods Within* (SPCK, London, 1992).
8. B. Chatwin, *The Songlines* (Jonathan Cape, London, 1987).
9. M. Fox, *The Coming of the Cosmic Christ, the Healing of Mother Earth and the Birth of Global Renaissance* (Harper and Row, New York, 1988).
10. G. Carey, 'Half a Gospel', *Church of England Newspaper*, 20 July 1990.
11. J. E. Lovelock, *Gaia* (Oxford University Press, Oxford, 1979).
12. *Resurgence*, Sept./Oct. 1990.
13. Bede, *A History of the English Church and People*, trans. L. Sherley-Price (Penguin Classics, Harmondsworth, 1962).
14. *The Deer's Cry – A Treasury of Irish Religious Verse*, ed. P. Murray (Four Courts Press, Dublin, 1986).

CHAPTER FOUR

Sacred Suffering

NO PERSON, and no community, can journey through life
without meeting with suffering. Any religion, then, which does
not take suffering seriously is not worth a moment's attention.
The problem of suffering, and the suffering of the innocent in
particular, is perhaps the basic issue of the religious quest.

When Prince Siddhartha Gautama, in the midst of his prosper-
ous, contented, pious life woke up to the fact that suffering is an
inevitable part of the human condition, he left palace and family
and travelled on a journey of faith through the great religious
traditions of his day, finding that none of them satisfied him in
giving an adequate response to the problem of suffering and
death. Eventually after a long period of thought and meditation
he named the Four Noble Truths which lie at the heart of
Buddhism – the religion which emerged from his spiritual quest.
They are:

1. Life and the world are imperfect, impermanent, generally
   unsatisfactory and inseparable from suffering.
2. The basic cause is selfish desire, the craving of the self for its
   own satisfaction.
3. The cause can be removed by any person.
4. The inadequacies and disappointments of life may be elimin-
   ated by the system of physical, moral and spiritual training
   known as the Noble Eightfold Path: right views, right motives,
   right speech, right action, right livelihood, right effort, right
   mindfulness and right absorption. The use of the word 'right'
   means whole, complete, flawless, untarnished.[1]

Other religious faiths have come up with different responses
to suffering and death. The Old Testament biblical writers

generally took a corporate view. Their dilemma might be expressed like this, 'Why do so many bad things keep happening to us?' The fact is that most of the history of Israel was one of suffering and disaster. A rational geo-historical explanation can be given for this – Israel was situated in a part of the world where great empires constantly touched, overlapped and fought. It was the Belgium of the ancient world – every army seemed to go through it. One after another each power became ascendant – Egypt, Assyria, Babylon, Persia, Greece, Rome. And the leaders of Israel had to come to terms with them. There were brief times of peace when there was a power vacuum (one such time occurred in the century before Jesus Christ's birth), but mostly Israel was caught in the vice of great power competition. War, suffering and confusion were the norm rather than the exception in the history of Israel.

This geo-historical explanation for the nation's woes would not have occurred to the biblical thinkers and if it had it would not have appealed. Their world-view was far more God-centred and saw the movement of early nations and powers as being in part manifestations of the divine will. The God who had called the people of Israel out of slavery in Egypt could not only move the hearts of Israel's leaders, but could harden the heart of Pharaoh or soften the heart of Cyrus the Mede in order to bend the events of history to his will.

The standard biblical answer, then, to the question 'Why do bad things keep happening to us?' was 'Because we are disobedient and faithless. We trust in our own power, or the power of our neighbours, instead of in the righteousness of God.'

Two later Old Testament writers were not, however, satisfied with this standard answer. In the Book of Job, the problem of innocent suffering was personalized. From the way the story is told there is no question that Job was a good, pious, God-fearing man who did everything that God required of him. And yet, in a story having echoes of the Greek pantheon, God allowed Satan to test him by loading suffering upon him. Job's friends sought to comfort him by giving him the standard religious explanations for his suffering, but Job's integrity was such that he rejected these – he knew that they were not adequate to explain his condition. Finally God intervened and gave Job a good dressing-down. In effect God said, 'Who do you think you are to question the way I run things?' This conclusion is surely a step forward. It acknowledges that there are no easy explanations for human suffering and that any which are given are likely to be wrong or inadequate. At the same time it answers the paradox 'Why and how does a loving and righteous God allow suffering?' with the answer, 'Trust God.'

Second Isaiah wrestled with the problem of innocent suffering in a way which proved to be very influential in Jesus' self-understanding (Isa 42). He was not content merely to trust God and leave the problem of suffering as a mystery. He developed the notion of the suffering servant, in which the willing suffering of the innocent became a way in which the life of a people was transformed and redemption was brought. Far from the suffering of the innocent being a tragic scandal, in willing co-operation with God it became the key which opened up the future of a people.

It is this understanding which gives Christians the backcloth to the ministry of Jesus Christ and it came to its high point in the Cross/resurrection stories. St Paul then developed it further for Christians of all times by teaching in the first chapter of his letter to the Colossians that 'I rejoice in my sufferings for your sake, and in my flesh I complete what is lacking in Christ's afflictions for the sake of his body, the Church' (Col 1.24). So the sufferings of the believer can be handled positively by being understood as sharing in the innocent suffering of Jesus, which in turn was the key which brought transformation and redemption to a lost and wounded world. But the theoretical understanding of the most devout follower of a religion may be transformed by personal experience.

C. S. Lewis wrote two books addressing the problem of suffering. The first, *The Problem of Pain*,[2] was written in the 1940s and is a sophisticated and helpful examination of the human and theological issues surrounding suffering; but it was written with the cool detachment of an Oxford academic writer. The second book is very different. It was written towards the end of C. S. Lewis's life after, to the astonishment of his colleagues, he had fallen in love with a lively American woman several years younger than himself. She developed cancer and during one of the periods of intermission in the disease they married. Their happiness was intense but brief. *A Grief Observed*[3] is Lewis's moving account of his own response to the death of his wife. It is less sophisticated than his earlier book, less elegant and less carefully argued. There is no doubt, however, that to a person facing the confusion, pain and fear, the suffering consequent upon bereavement, *A Grief Observed* is a real, useful sharing, coming from a man who knew his need, who because of what he had been through had cast away religious certainties in his longing to scream at God and at the same time to trust God.

In the Christian tradition suffering, whilst not being sought, is not to be avoided or explained away. The poorest, weakest and most vulnerable communities and people, and those who suffer in any society, are very often those who are open and generous, loving, brave and spirit-filled. One cannot read the gospel stories without gaining the impression that Jesus had a preference for the poor and needy. And conversely the poor and suffering people were the majority of those who went to Jesus because they knew their need of help and of God. The grace of God may well be available for all people at all times, but it is those who know their need of it for whom it is most likely to be a vivid reality. Because of Jesus' preference for the poor and suffering and his attention to healing their wounds, Christianity has always taught that Christians should give similar attention to the vulnerable and see in them the vulnerability of Christ.

Verrier Elwin, who lived and worked with the tribal people of Assam for many years, expresses this understanding in the following poem.[4]

THE CHILD AND THE ROOD

A baby girl, not six years old,
Dwells in the distant hills:
Her timid eyes already hold
Their share of human ills.

No school for her: already now
She works from early dawn,
And runs to catch the vagrant cow
Or grinds the stubborn corn.

Of sweets she hardly knows the taste,

No toy she'll ever see;
A scanty rag about her waist
Is her sole finery.

And once I saw her stagger home
Beneath a load of wood
Laid on her head, so burdened that
I thought upon the Rood.

Before that little child I saw
The form of one who bowed
Beneath another load, and walked
Amidst an angry crowd.

Verrier Elwin lived in India in the 1930s, but a recent visit to the tribal people of Orissa has brought home to us the shameful fact that their situation has not changed significantly.

Christianity is not alone in seeing a close affinity between God and those suffering pain or poverty. Muslims see the care of the poor and needy as a vital religious duty. The third pillar of the faith is *zakat*, the act of giving a set proportion of one's wealth each year to help the needy and to support good causes. Fasting during Ramadan reminds Muslims of the month in which Muhammad received special revelations and also helps them to develop self-discipline and an attitude of generosity toward others. The Qur'an teaches: 'Righteousness is . . . [that he] gives his wealth, out of love for Him, for kinsmen, orphans, the needy, the traveller, those who ask, and to ransom captives.'

The Bengali author, Rabindranath Tagore, was a writer, poet, artist and musician from the Hindu tradition. He was the thirteenth child of a holy man, Maharshi Debendranath, and from him inherited an inclination to austerity. When he arrived in the West in 1912, Ezra Pound said that he made him feel 'like a painted Pict with a stone war-club'.[5] Within a year Tagore had become the first Asian to win the Nobel Prize for Literature. Between 1913 and 1930 he gave hundreds of addresses in universities around the world, but his ideals of education, centred in performance, art and rural life, were best developed in his international 'universal university' of Shantiniketan, founded in 1921. There he chose to live in an ordinary village house and to have built as university accommodation the thatch-roofed and clay houses lived in by most of India's poor people. He wrote:

Here is thy footstool and there rest thy feet where live the poorest,
and lowliest, and lost.

When I try to bow to thee, my obeisance cannot reach down to the
depth where thy feet rest among the poorest, and lowliest, and lost.

Pride can never approach to where thou walkest in the clothes of the
humble among the poorest, and lowliest, and lost.

My heart can never find its way to where thou keepest company with
the companionless among the poorest, the lowliest, and the lost.[6]

Sogyal Rinpoche, writing to enlighten Western readers on
Tibetan Buddhism, has given invaluable advice on how to
awaken love and compassion which may eventually become
boundless, including not only the whole universe but people we
dislike or even hate. He has suggested that we go back in our
thoughts, as far as it is necessary to go, to recreate an experience
of love and to dwell upon a person who loved us and the
happiness this gave us. We are advised to remember a particularly
vivid experience of love, to feel grateful and self-consciously
to love the person who loved us, so that little by little we become
aware of being worthy of love. We may then give love, beginning
with those closest to us and extending by degrees outwards to
friends, acquaintances, neighbours, and then to strangers and the
people we may call enemies, until finally we embrace the whole
universe.[7]

No people are in greater need of this understanding than the
Tibetan people themselves, because they have faced enmity,
war, death, torture and exile since their country was invaded by
China in 1950. Buddhism has been the religion of Tibet from
the time when Buddhist masters were invited there in the
seventh century CE. In the seventeenth century CE, Buddhist
monks became the rulers of Tibet and the present Dalai Lama
is the fourteenth such ruler. After the 1950 invasion the post-
war Communist regime systematically destroyed the Tibetan
culture and heritage, especially the monasteries and temples.
Unspeakable atrocities were meted out to the Tibetan people
and well over a million of them have died. Those who survived
have vivid stories to tell of suffering, starvation and deprivation. One, called Norbu Karsip, told how he was imprisoned
for twenty-three years, during which time torture was often a
daily occurrence. His shoulders were dislocated through having
his hands tied behind his back and then being suspended by the

hands from the ceiling. Thin sharpened bamboo sticks with miniature Chinese flags were inserted under his finger-nails, and he was forced to stand with raised arms so that the flags fluttered in the wind.[8]

Given this experience it is surprising that many of the Tibetan people living in India, including the Dalai Lama, are patient, peaceful, and seemingly without bitterness, building up their faith and culture as best they can in new places, and giving loving and compassionate attention to the hundreds of babies and children who are orphaned. 'Tibet will not die because there is no death for the human spirit.'[9]

The Dalai Lama himself is a well-known world-wide religious leader who works for justice and peace not only for his own people but for all. He stands in the fine tradition of Tibetan Buddhism which embraces the ideal of the *Bodhisattva*, the one who has gained enlightenment but who renounces final entry into Nirvana in order to relieve suffering in the world.

> If I do not exchange my happiness
> For the suffering of others,
> I shall not attain the state of buddhahood,
> And even in samsara
> I shall have no real joy.[10]

Avalokiteshvara is the Buddha of compassion, often represented in Tibetan iconography as having a thousand eyes to behold the wretchedness in all corners of the universe, and a thousand loving arms to reach out to all the wretched.

Perhaps the poorest city on the face of the earth, and yet a 'City of Joy', is Calcutta. Brother André of the L'Arche Community wrote,

Once you know Calcutta you can never leave it for good. There is that strange attraction, the immense crowd of paupers, a city of death and of life. It is a triumph of life over death, masses of derelicts, alive and smiling, sleeping and lamenting. A city where great love exists between people. The poor are good to the poor, so many acts of charity, of mutual help, of kindness; so many who are in a state of misery, but who forget their misery to help one who is more miserable yet.[11]

Brother André was writing twenty years ago but Calcutta has changed little. The streets are still grim and the paintless and dilapidated buildings loom large. Even worse than it must have been twenty years ago is the pollution, for, although many of the poor still pull rickshaws, the number of cars has increased. Traffic jams are a huge problem and the air is thick with fumes. Some of the Calcutta residents told us that they have perpetual sore throats and that Calcutta has the highest incidence of cancer in the world. The 'immense crowd of paupers' is bigger than it was twenty years ago, and people are dying at every minute of the day and night. In Mother Teresa's home for the dying and destitute, as people die they are immediately replaced by a constant stream of other dying people and so on, seemingly forever. The saving grace is that the people who die in Mother Teresa's home do so in peace, surrounded by love.

However, the most noisy and dusty Calcutta street may lead, often through a grubby doorway and a dark, dank stairway, to a hive of faith-filled, loving and dedicated activity. An unpromising doorway led us up to the 'Silence' community of those who 'can neither hear nor speak except visually and others who cannot go places except in their imaginations and yet who aspire towards self-sufficiency'. The handicapped people work together to earn a living producing greeting cards, incense sticks, candles, jewellery and wooden decorations. Silence was started in the early 1980s by a small group of deaf artists who came together to produce the hand-painted cards. The organization now offers a wide variety of employment opportunities to seventy-two deaf and dumb, blind and otherwise disabled people. Perhaps just as significantly, there is a sense of purpose and community in the overcrowded work-rooms. But the major battle of finding these disabled young people creative work in the outside world is still to be fought by Silence.[12]

The Indian Council of Sport for the Disabled similarly exhibits a shabby exterior, but once inside the building the visitor is taken aback by the atmosphere of love and service, cultivated over sixteen years of painstaking and dedicated work by Tapan Dhar and his co-workers. Tapan is himself disabled and from a base of weakness and disadvantage he has built up an organization through which over seventeen thousand disabled people are enrolled with the Council. Seminars and conferences are organized, advice is given, skills are taught and handicrafts are being developed. Opportunities are offered in sporting activities, including those at the international level.

Brother André wrote that 'the poor are good to the poor'. Jean Vanier's life changed when he realized that the poor are not only good for the poor, but they are good for everybody else as well. It is now well over twenty-five years since Jean Vanier left his professional work as a teacher of philosophy and founded the now world-wide L'Arche communities. He began by inviting Raphael and Philip, both mentally handicapped, to live with him in a small house in Trosly-Breuil in France. Jean began with the idea of helping Raphael and Philip to become part of the village, but he soon realized that he himself had benefited more than he could say, in learning what he called a new language, 'the language of the heart'.

From those who are very small, very broken, very wounded, comes life ... We can turn away, and retreat into our own world; or we can walk towards those in pain. Then something is born in us – compassion – and maybe we discover the great gift of the poor – that they reveal our own poverty.[13]

We have often been inspired and have learnt from the power of disabled and seemingly weak people. Sarah was severely disabled at birth, but her brain is undamaged, and she writes inspiring poetry from her struggle for life and hope. Joan, who is severely disabled by cerebral palsy, has been decorated for her work over many years of organizing and supervising a holiday programme for disabled children in London. Jane is blind and is the director of a charitable society which cares for elderly and disabled people in one London borough. Jill has epileptic fits and is crippled with arthritis. She works full-time in an office, and in her spare time she makes costumes for an amateur dramatic society and studies for an Open University degree. Mike was badly damaged at birth and grew up knowing that he would always struggle to speak to others and that he would never walk. As he grew he learnt to express himself by writing his feelings down, he thought a lot and began to write poetry which was inspiring. He had a book of poetry published before he died in his early twenties.[14]

What Valerie had feared for a long time happened to her. After her operation she was told that she had extensive stomach cancer and she went back alone to her small flat. Her sister and friends came to visit her occasionally, bringing flowers and plants. Her most trusted friend was the nurse who looked in every day. She could talk to her for as long as she needed to, sharing her worries and her sadness. She had been a hard-working teacher and now she focused on the telephone number of her nurse and managed to be positive and even cheerful at times. Gradually Valerie could not eat very much and she entered a hospice where the care and love for her continued, so that she was able to die talking of her death as her 'last great adventure'.

The theologian John Robinson died of cancer in 1983. His book *Honest to God* caused a storm when it was published in 1962 whilst he was still Bishop of Woolwich. During the rest of his life, as well as publishing scholarly theological books, he also produced a stream of popular books and articles, opening up the fruits of modern scholarship to the general, non-specialist reader. His belief that 'God was in the rapids as much as on the rocks' struck a chord in the mind-set of British society in the 1960s and 1970s. The honesty which he had displayed in these theological writings was displayed in a moving and personal way when he discovered that he was suffering from cancer. Before he died, he wrote and spoke of his impending death and of his awareness of God, the God of surprise and the God of truth, the God in all things who is 'to be found in the cancer as much as in the sunset'.[15]

Richard de Zoysa was one of Sri Lanka's best-known journalists and TV personalities. He was snatched from his mother's house and tortured and killed in 1990. His body was washed up on the beach several days after he was killed. His mother, Dr Manorani Savaranamuttu, later said,

'The sea brought my son back to me. I think sometimes in the night that God couldn't save my son, but the sea brought him back to me so that I could fight.' And fight she did, drawing the attention of the whole world to what had happened to her son and to many others. Her grief galvanised her into dignified action for justice and for future peace in her country. She said, 'When we were children everything was fair, everything was beautiful. We played on the beaches and no bodies came, we drove to the hills, we skipped, we laughed, we learned. Nobody came to kill us. So do not we, because we had that youth, owe it to our children to get up and fight? So that they may know the same peace, the same happiness of youth, and not be killed like dogs, to float down rivers, washed up by the sea.'[16]

It seems a mystery that some people are crushed by their troubles and even blame God, whilst others, equally oppressed, fight spiritedly. For example, two old ladies, both members of the same London parish, were mugged. Lily was mugged in the park. She was pushed to the side of the path and robbed of everything in her handbag, including a small amount of money. She refused to be comforted by the church members and said, over and over again, 'Why are people like that? I feel very bitter.' Doris is in her mid-eighties and still keeps a beautiful garden. One day, as she was gardening, two youths stopped her and asked her if they could help to carry the tools into the house. As they entered the house they threw Doris against the edge of the table, took a significant amount of money, drawn out from her account to pay a builder, and ran. When she was visited in hospital Doris, whilst naturally worried about the loss of her money, was also concerned about her attackers, 'We must pray for those young men,' she said.

Courage and inspiration sometimes come from surprising sources. Betty lives in a South Yorkshire town. She is lame and in her seventies. Not very long ago she opened her front door, only to be attacked so badly that she had to spend a long time in hospital. As she lay in her hospital bed she almost felt she would give in, but a book she had read kept coming into her mind, telling her to 'get up and fight'. She made a conscious decision to fight and to strive to recover her health, and she did recover. The passage which inspired her came from the *Bhagavad Gita*, part of the *Mahabarata*, and perhaps the most well-known of the Hindu scriptures:

> Arise, O son of Kunti and fight!
> Look upon pleasure and pain, victory and defeat with an
> equal eye.
> Make ready for the combat and thou shalt commit no sin.[17]

The *Bhagavad Gita*, the 'Song of the Lord', is a song of the partnership of the generous grace of God with struggling humanity, and it seems that this partnership is only possible when people are struggling and so desperate that they will at last listen to God. In the story Arjuna, the warrior, is in despair and does not want to fight but he is given courage and hope by his conversations with Lord Krishna.

One way Krishna challenges Arjuna to conquer his despair is by focusing on God in 'a single oneness of pure love, of never-straying love for me; retiring to solitary places, and avoiding the noisy multitudes.'[18] There are those whose 'retirement to solitary places' has been compulsory. Walter and Albertina Sisulu recently revisited Robben Island, where Walter Sisulu had been a prisoner for twenty years, and had thought he would be a prisoner for life. He and the other prisoners received family visits only every six months and Albertina Sisulu had to travel overnight by train, sleeping in Cape Town station, and then take a ferry to the island for her half-hour of non-contact conversation with her husband. On the boat going back to the mainland after their return visit Walter Sisulu said that being on the island had not been a wasted time. Even the work he and other prisoners, including Nelson Mandela, had had to do, such as digging in the lime quarry, had been used as an opportunity to hold discussions on politics and economics and to plan the future. Now the task was to build that future and not to waste time being bitter against those who had been the persecutors.

Marango Bando was imprisoned in Malawi for two years because she came to Britain for the Mothers' Union World-Wide Council against the wishes of Dr Banda's government. She was detained two days after her return to Malawi, and no reason was given. She shows no bitterness against those who imprisoned her, even though she is diabetic and could easily have died in prison. Today she is playing her part in building a now-democratic country.

To Western eyes it may seem surprising that many people of other cultures give priority to their religious faith and practice in situations of overwhelming deprivation. It is amazing that refugees should seek a place where they can worship long before they obtain secure accommodation for themselves, but that is what has happened recently in the Sudan. A civil war has been going on for more than ten years now and about one-and-a-half million people have died. The reasons for the long tale of suffering and struggle are many, including, it is claimed, the colonial failure to develop the whole country, creating rather a dominant North, which continued when the independent government was established in Khartoum in 1956. The South has great economic potential, however. 'If you drop a nail into

the ground it will flower by morning.' Oil has also been discovered, but the war has reduced the South to extreme poverty
where people 'wait like beggars for aid and think a rat is a good
meal'.[19]

Bishop Seme Solomona and his people left their homes in Yei
in 1990, and in 1994 they again left their temporary homes
in Kaya, in the face of the approaching fighting between the
Sudanese Government and the SPLA troops. The border barrier
between Sudan and Uganda was lifted on 5 August 1994,
and the people began to move across in their hundreds. Bishop
Seme Solomona later spoke of the evacuation of Kaya. 'It was
just like the children of Israel leaving Egypt,' he said. The people
streamed out of Kaya, across the bridge and into Uganda. The
road was solidly packed with possibly fifty thousand people
including the war-wounded, elderly and mothers with young
children. Two babies were born on that difficult journey. As
the people arrived in Koboka in Uganda the rain poured down
and they shivered under trees before they could move into
transit camps in the bush, where they had to cut down trees to
make rough shelters. A stream provided water but it rapidly
became polluted as well over twenty thousand people used it
for drinking and washing. Ten days after the evacuation,
supplies began to get through and stronger shelters were erected,
with several families sharing one shelter, and people asked
where they would worship and set to work to provide a worship
place. The story has echoes of King David's challenge to his
people in the Second Book of Samuel as he settled in Jerusalem,
'See now I dwell in a house of cedar, but the ark of God dwells
in a tent' (2 Sam 7.2). The Sudanese refugees were not so
fortunate as to have solid houses themselves, but nevertheless
they wanted to provide a proper space for the worship of God.
We read of 'a hopeful and confident mood in the camps . . . The
people of Kaya, far from being demoralized and depressed . . .
are hopeful and confident of God's presence with them.'[20]

The thin, sometimes invisible, line between human hope and
dehumanizing despair, between standing up fighting and sitting
down weeping, was perhaps seen at its starkest in the reactions
of those caught up as victims in the horror of the Nazi concentration camps. Sarah always felt a deep and abiding sadness
because her father, a respected and proud man, had died in

helplessness and anguish in the Dachau concentration camp during World War II. In the spring of 1994 Sarah received a telephone call at her home in Israel from a Lithuanian who told her that he had been with her father when he died and that he would like to meet her. Sarah agreed to meet the man and began the conversation by referring to the sadness of her father's degradation. The man was astonished, saying that he did not know what she was talking about. Her father had in no way been degraded but had died a dignified and courageous death. As a doctor he had been asked by the camp authorities to choose the people who were well enough to work. He had refused and had gone on hunger strike as a protest against the abomination of the camp and its horrors. Sarah learnt that her father had in fact chosen his own death, that he had deliberately died for the people around him. She has felt enormous happiness since learning the truth. Her father's story was one of dignity, power and triumph after all.

Sarah moved from sadness to joy when she learnt the truth about her father, that he had not died in despair but purposefully, even proudly. When we read gospel accounts of Jesus dying on the cross it seems clear that his followers moved from despair to hope as they began to see that, far from being merely a victim, forsaken, defeated and directionless, Jesus had in an act of free will become a powerful and positive agent, dramatically linking earth and heaven, human beings and God, and challenging us all, as he challenged Mary Magdalene after he rose from the dead, to stop clinging and weeping and to go and share the good news.

And lest it be thought that life out of death is mere religious wish-fulfilment, even hard-headed rationalists such as the philosopher Sir Alfred Ayer have been disturbed by near-death experiences, now becoming increasingly common as modern medicine succeeds in frequently plucking people back from the edge of the grave.

When he was seventy-seven years old Sir Alfred's heart stopped for four minutes in a London hospital. He wrote a two-thousand-word account of the experience. It includes the following:

I was confronted by a red light, exceedingly bright and also very painful even when I turned away from it. I was aware that this light was responsible for the government of the universe. Among its ministers were two creatures who had been put in charge of space . . . space was slightly out of joint . . . I felt it was up to me to put things right . . . attempts to communicate with the guardians of the universe elicited no response. I became more and more desperate until the experience suddenly came to an end.

Ayer summed up his experience by saying that, though his atheism was intact, the experience 'slightly weakened my conviction that my genuine death . . . will be the end of me, though I continue to hope it will be.'[21]

Scientific and medical explanations for the phenomena found in near-death experiences have been produced, but what is perhaps the most pervasive after-effect lies in the changed attitude to death of those who have had such an experience. Commonly, they have lost their fear of death and they have tended to find that they have an enhanced appreciation of beauty, silence and 'the sanctity of the present moment'. Their concern for others is greater; material values and status matter less; there is a new quest for meaning and for intellectual or spiritual understanding. All in all there are interesting parallels with the reported effects of mystical experiences whether in the 'silence of the desert' or in the 'oneness of creation'. It would be wrong to look to these near-death experiences as giving any evidence for life after death, but they reinforce the fact that whether we give sacred or secular interpretations to our common human experiences, suffering and death remain profound mysteries where strength and weakness, joy and pain, hope and despair are all part of the warp and weft. In the face of such mysteries perhaps silence is the best response, and it is with 'sacred silence' that we now engage. But first let us ponder two further insights which from very different traditions and perspectives bring a message of hope in the heart of suffering.

From the Hasidic Jewish tradition comes the story of the Sorrow Tree. On the Day of Judgement, the story goes, each person will be allowed to hang all of his or her unhappiness on a branch of the great Tree of Sorrows. After everyone has dangled their sorrows from the limbs they may all walk slowly around the tree. Each has to search for a preferable set of sorrows. In the end, however, each person freely chooses to reclaim his or her own personal set of sorrows rather than those of another. Each leaves the tree a more thoughtful and wiser person.[22]

Then from the Christian tradition come words written by P. T. Forsyth at a grim hour during World War I.

Heaven does not laugh loud but it laughs last – when all the world will laugh in its light. It is an irony gentler and more patient than the bending skies, the irony of a long love and the play of its sure mastery; it is the smile of the holy in its silent omnipotence of mercy. The non-intervention of God bears very heavy interest, and He is greatly to be feared when He does nothing. He moves in great orbits, out of sight and sound, but He always arrives. The world gets a long time to pay, but all the accounts are kept – to the uttermost farthing. Lest if anything were forgotten there might be something unforgiven, unredeemed and unholy still.[23]

NOTES

1. W. Rahula, *What the Buddha Taught* (Gordon Fraser, London, 1978).
2. C. S. Lewis, *The Problem of Pain* (Fontana Books, London, 1940).
3. C. S. Lewis, *A Grief Observed* (Faber and Faber, London, 1961).
4. V. Elwin, *Twenty-Eight Poems* (Private publication).
5. K. Dutta and A. Robinson, *Rabindranath Tagore: The Myriad Minded Man* (Bloomsbury, London, 1995).
6. R. Tagore, *Gitanjali* (Papermac, London, 1986).
7. Sogyal Rinpoche, *The Tibetan Book of Living and Dying*, eds P. Gaffney and A. Harvey (Rider, London, 1992).
8. M. Craig, *Tears of Blood. A Cry for Tibet* (HarperCollins, London, 1992).
9. Professor P. Sharma, *People of the Prayer Wheel* (Dharamsala).
10. *Shantideva*, trans. S. Bachelor (Library of Tibetan Works and Archives, Dharamsala, 1979).
11. S. Mosteller, *My Brother, My Sister* (Griffin House, Toronto, 1974).
12. A. Collins, 'Silence Speaks', *Christians Aware Magazine*, Summer 1994.
13. J. Vanier, *The Tablet*, 20 January 1990.
14. The Crypt Foundation, Forum, Stirling Road, Chichester, W. Sussex.
15. E. James, *A Life of Bishop John A. T. Robinson, Scholar, Pastor, Prophet* (Collins, London, 1987).
16. *Out of the Depths – Struggle and Hope in Sri Lanka* (Christians Aware, Leicester, 1992).
17. *Bhagavad Gita – the Gospel of the Lord Shri Krishna*, trans. Shri Purohit Swami (Faber and Faber, London, 1978), chapter 2.
18. Ibid.
19. A. Allam, *Sudan – An Untold Story* (Beaminster Team Publications, 1992).
20. S. and A. Wheeler, letter to CMS, 15 August 1994.

21. Interview with John Edge, 'Friday people', *Guardian*, 1988.
22. S. Kopp, *If You Meet the Buddha on the Road Kill Him!* (Sheldon Press, London, 1974).
23. David Edwards, *God's Cross in Our World* (SCM Press, London, 1968).

CHAPTER FIVE

Sacred Silence

Lord, it is night.
The night is for stillness.
Let us be still in the presence of God.

It is a night after a long day.
What has been done has been done;
What has not been done has not been done,
Let it be.

The night is dark.
Let our fears of the darkness of the
World and of our own lives
Rest in you.

The night is quiet.
Let the quietness of your peace enfold us,
All dear to us,
And all who have no peace.

The night heralds the dawn.
Let us look expectantly to a new day,
New joys, new possibilities.

In your name we pray. Amen.
(From the New Zealand Prayer Book)

The quest for silence and solitude is natural to human beings, and need not necessarily be associated with religion. One popular twentieth-century way of seeking silence is to go fishing, and sometimes the fisherfolk, huddled over their rods and lines around a lake or along a canal, look as though they have taken over from medieval monks and nuns in their chosen, though temporary, solitude. Throughout human history, however, silence has been most passionately sought along the path of faith.

The meeting with God in solitary places and especially in desert places runs throughout the Old Testament from the time of Moses' great journeys with his people. John the Baptist is one of the more colourful characters in the New Testament. He was certainly influenced by and perhaps had been a member of the Essene community, which lived a disciplined life of silence, prayer, celibacy and study on the fringes of the desert. We read of John in the first verses of St Mark's Gospel, 'one crying in the wilderness. Prepare the way of the Lord . . . ' John was the forerunner of Jesus the Christ who went into the wilderness to prepare for his coming ministry after being baptized by John, and throughout that ministry went away into quiet places from time to time. This pattern was also followed by Christian hermits down the ages to the present day.

The early Church, which had known persecution at the hands of the Roman Empire, was soon embraced by it, becoming the 'official' religion. First persecution and later populism led many Christians to move to remote places; the most popular was Egypt, where the desert was easy to reach and where there were many caves. It was not long before the Egyptian monastic communities and hermits were quite famous. People journeyed to visit them and the popularity of the solitary life spread throughout Europe. One story of Antony of Egypt is that he so inspired people to flock to the desert that he could not cope with them when they arrived, and ran away, making the journey of over a hundred miles to an oasis in the mountains near the Red Sea, where he spent the rest of his life in solitude, only emerging to give occasional advice to local hermits.

St Antony seems to have managed to love God with all his heart, but he found it more difficult to enjoy the company of his neighbours. This combination of love of solitude with God or nature and impatience with the presence of human beings was shared by St Cuthbert, the great monk of Lindisfarne, who 'longed for a desert in the sea', an island where he could be alone with God. He went to Inner Farne where he lived alone and prayed, with just the seals and the sea birds for company.[1]

It is not only religious saints who have this disposition. The fell-walker and writer, Arthur Wainwright, who delighted in mountains and being in them, and whose guides to the Lakeland Fells have attracted thousands of people to the Lake

District, himself felt driven deliberately to avoid the best-known areas. There are many stories of him refusing to speak to people when he was out walking alone, and of him choosing quiet times and obscure routes, even climbing mountains after dark and sometimes spending the night on a summit so that he could remain alone. He was greatly inspired by mountainous scenery and he shared his vision in his drawings and writings and, rarely, in communications with his fellow walkers, most of whom he seems rather to have despised. The walkers he disliked the most were those who went to the mountains for physical exercise, 'without seeing anything but the track before them. Mountains are there to be enjoyed, and enjoyed leisurely . . . '[2]

And lest it be thought that solitude is only to be found in the great outdoors, in deserts, on islands or mountains, the poet Philip Larkin speaks of solitude in more mundane surroundings.

BEST SOCIETY

> . . . I lock my door.
> The gas-fire breathes. The wind outside
> Ushers in evening rain. Once more
> Uncontradicting solitude
> Supports me on its giant palm;
> And like a sea-anemone
> Or simple snail, there cautiously
> Unfolds, emerges, what I am.[3]

The Egyptian monks, hermits and those in communities were mainly silent because they were listening for the direction of God towards the Kingdom and did not wish to waste time, as they saw it, in worldly pursuits and conversations. They believed that the qualities of the Kingdom of God, love, joy and peace, were more likely to be built by silence and by listening to and respecting others than by words which led to arguments and bitterness. One piece of advice was, 'If you do not find peace, why do you speak? Be silent, and when a conversation takes place, prefer to listen rather than to talk.' A brother asked Abba Poemen, 'How should I behave in my cell in the place where I am living?' The reply was, 'Behave as if you were a stranger, and wherever you are, do not expect your words to have any influence and you will be at peace.'[4]

In Hinduism Sri Aurobindo moved from a noisy and activist role in Indian politics into four years of silent yoga in Pondicherry, from which he emerged in 1914 to share his message of God everywhere and in everything. He believed that God was only hidden because people did not take trouble to find him. He worked for forty years to help create 'a divine life upon earth', at the same time being very aware of what was actually happening around him. He saw the aim and goal of silent meditation as being the search for God and the finding of God; and for him this was the only way to live, a delight and true love in which participants would naturally move towards God as God moved naturally towards them. He believed that awareness of the divine reality would lead to awareness of the same reality in other people and other cultures and religions, to an awareness that all people are vehicles of God on earth, and essentially bound together in unity. How could such realization lead to anything other than co-operation and love, the coming of the divine kingdom upon the earth?

> Behind all eyes I meet thy secret gaze
> And in each voice I hear thy magic tune:
> Thy sweetness haunts my heart through Nature's ways;
> Nowhere it beats now from thy snare immune.
>
> It loves Thy body in all living things;
> Thy joy is there in every leaf and stone:
> The moments bring Thee on their fiery wings;
> Sight's endless artistry is Thou alone.
>
> Time voyages with Thee upon its prow –
> And all the future's passionate hope is Thou.
>
> Sri Aurobindo[5]

We visited the Sri Aurobindo ashram in Bangalore, a place of peace and beauty which, like his ashram in Pondicherry, is a place of quiet acceptance of a vast assortment of people who work out their future vocations and lifestyles for themselves. The ashrams are characterized by their affirmation of the world and of every aspect of life, in the belief that there is no part of life that may not be orientated to the divine. The challenge to seekers is towards being transfigured within the world rather than to being on the edge of or outside worldly concerns and issues. The ashram in Pondicherry includes farms, workshops and an international education centre which caters for every level and every aspect of education from engineering to dancing. Students learn by listening and by quietly working things out for themselves.

We see this pattern of silent prayer within the traditions of most religions. Hinduism recognizes that seeking God in solitude is an essential part of the journey of faith from its beginnings, through all its stages to its end. The true seeker is the one who demands nothing of God, but simply to be with him; the one who does not judge the world and its people or struggle to change them, but who is ready, in quiet but energetic peacefulness, to help when needed. And God is sought in the transcendent and within each person.

The Hindu tradition understands the great spaces of the world and of the cosmos as no bigger and no more important or inspiring than the space within the heart, 'The little space within the heart is as great as this vast universe . . . for the whole universe is in Him and He dwells within our heart.'[6] Ramana Maharshi, born in 1879, was a sage of Tiruvanamalai in South India who communicated through silence and look. He taught that self-understanding and surrender to God were the only way to live. Many people spoke of encountering God through him.

The spiritual methods by which this 'little space within the heart' is to be found lie in the disciplines of meditation and contemplation. The eagle, it seems, has a remarkable eye. As the bird soars high above the earth it has a wide-angled vision and a comprehensive view to the horizon on every side. But it also has a number of cells at the centre of its retina which focus upon the particular. This means that it can, at the same time as having a general overall vision, focus very narrowly and precisely. The slightest movement of the smallest mouse on the earth below does not miss its attention. Meditation offers the opportunity for developing a similar bi-focal vision. Silence and concentration are at its heart; it starts with ways of developing a wide-angled love which watches and observes without clinging, and then it moves to a more single-minded concentration or contemplation, focusing the soul on matters of God.

The religious symbol of the mandala has enabled people of very different cultures to approach meditatively the 'world in a grain of sand'. In the Hindu tradition one form of the mandala represents the space of the cosmos and the space within the heart. At the centre is the presence of God, not merely outside and beyond, but the core of all that is, linked to all that is. A Hindu creation myth tells that the god Brahma, standing on a thousand-petalled lotus, turned to the four points of the compass to take his bearings before beginning to create. Carl Jung, the Swiss psychologist, saw this as an orientation exercise, symbolic of the human need for psychic orientation.[7]

Mandalas are very ancient symbols and aids to contemplation which still occur in most faiths. They are often either circular or square with a clear and dynamic link of the outer edges to the centre. Many mandalas are of a flower, usually a lotus in the East, or of a cross or a wheel. One Chinese Buddhist mandala is in the form of a pomegranate with a Buddha figure embracing wisdom at the centre and surrounded by two or three lesser divinities before circular drums on each petal. The outside of the petals also have deities and emblems, including a horse, an elephant and a wheel.

In the Christian tradition over the centuries, some who have seen the crucifix as a mandala have gazed at it for hours at a time, centring themselves in the profound self-giving love of God. The rose windows of medieval cathedrals may be seen as abstract mandalas, well worth gazing at in contemplative prayer in every generation. The early-seventeenth-century Dutch mystic Jacob Boehme produced fine mandalas. One of them shows the created and fallen world with the four elements and their associated misdeeds, all surrounded by the serpent of eternity. The whole circle relates to the centre which contains the weeping eye of God, the point from which the salvation of the whole world is possible, through love and compassion.

A mandala which holds elements of both Christian and Buddhist imagery is the cross in the lotus flower which is the badge of a Christian Buddhist Centre for dialogue in the New Territories near Hong Kong. The lotus flower growing out of the muddy stuff of human existence floats on the surface of the pond and unfolds its petals in the warmth of the sun. Thus the Buddhist sees the mindful soul floating free from the drama and distraction of the world and unfolding in the peace and bliss of nirvana. But the mandala to which we refer has a cross in the heart of the peaceful lotus, reminding us of the Christian tradition that, whilst we blossom and unfold in the warmth of God's love, true peace is to be found in self-sacrificial service.

In the Hindu tradition there is Yoga, which means linking or union, perhaps the most developed methodology of meditation and contemplation through the limbs. The practitioner believes that through Yoga the reality of God within the human heart is linked to the reality of God everywhere in the wide world. Even a simple greeting, with two palms pressed together and held near the heart, is a recognition of the God within and the God in the other person, people and beyond.

One branch of Yoga places great emphasis upon the use of the mantra, a sound, word or phrase repeated constantly to first still the mind and then re-focus it. A–U–M is the three-syllabled mantra which represents the mystery of the universe in both sound and vibration. The Upanishads explain it in trinitarian terms. One understanding is that the three rounded forms represent the structure of the universe in its emergence. They represent the A . . . U sound in its extension, whilst the M sound is represented as a dot without extension, the element which is beyond representation. AUM is the alpha and omega of existence, containing all possible sounds and even sound-lessness.

Jyoti Sahi, an Indian Christian writer, poet and artist, sometimes depicts the AUM as the Holy Spirit in the form of a dove. In one picture, for example, the dove with an olive branch flies over the three hills of the Trinity.[8]

The divine may be heard in sound or in silence, and often by moving from one to the other.

> The sound of Brahman is AUM. At the end of AUM there is silence. It is a silence of joy. It is the end of the journey where fear and sorrow are no more: steady, motionless, never-failing, everlasting, immortal. It is called the omnipresent Vishnu. In order to reach the highest, consider in adoration the sound and the silence of Brahman.[9]

This use of a mantra is a popular method of meditation in all religious traditions. In the Eastern Orthodox Christian tradition the Jesus Prayer, 'Lord Jesus Christ, Son of God, have mercy on me, a sinner', is constantly repeated, so stilling the mind and focusing the attention of the disciple upon Jesus. The use of mantra-type meditation is becoming generally valued in very different schools of Christian tradition today. The Prayer of Stillness of the Fellowship of Contemplative Prayer begins with the repetition of a sentence from the Bible. The Taizé Ecumenical Christian Community in Burgundy uses this method, moving from repetitive singing through a short biblical reading towards silent meditation followed by brief vocal prayers in different languages. At Taizé the silent meditation lasts for ten minutes at a time and it does not matter whether those taking part are two or three, gathered together in a tiny hut in the middle of a shanty town somewhere in the developing world, or thousands of young people in the huge and worship-filled church at Taizé itself. The gathered silence at Taizé is impressive, for calming the mind towards silence is not easy, as Arjuna pointed out in the *Bhagavad Gita*: 'The mind is fickle and turbulent, obstinate and strong, yea extremely difficult as the wind to control.'[10]

But the mastering of the fickle mind can be the key to authentic living. There is a story told of Confucius who once saw a man plunging into a raging torrent and then climbing out on the other side of the river singing. 'How did you do that?' Confucius asked the man. 'I plunge into the water with the whirl, and I come out with the whirl. I accommodate myself to the water and don't expect the water to accommodate itself to me.' Silent meditation through the traditions of the great religions is a powerful way of accommodating oneself to the realities of life and death.

The gathered silence of a Quaker meeting depends upon its members quietening their minds and trusting each other enough to listen to God, whilst at the same time trusting God as one who may be known. When words do arise in a meeting they are, so long as they come from the heart and not from the head, 'like the ripples on the surface of deep water'; they do not disturb but rather deepen the silence and awareness of community love and respect.[11]

The monks of the Carthusian order spend their lives 'speaking by silence'. They live in separate cells where they spend their lives in silence, growing and cooking their own food and only meeting for worship in the community church each evening. If Quaker words are 'ripples on the surface of deep water', a modern Carthusian writer talks of the daily irritations which come within this life of silence as 'the ruffling of the surface of the soul'.[12]

The value of silence and awareness has always been part of the

Buddhist tradition. Gautama Buddha left his palace home and spent six years in almost complete solitude before beginning his teaching within a community of monks and later nuns. Westerners in recent years have shown most interest in the form of Buddhism known as Zen Buddhism, and we have had the opportunity of visiting one of the large Buddhist monasteries in Japan where Zen Buddhism is taught. Zen is notoriously difficult to grasp or explain but it is best seen as a state of consciousness in which one sees into the essence of things. Zen is concerned with direct experience either of the intuition or by the senses. In either case the starting-point is the moving beyond thought.

Traditional Buddhist meditation puts great emphasis on 'mindfulness', through which the disciple learns to be aware of each moment of living rather than drifting though life with the mind in neutral. In the meditation hall the disciple is taught how to make friends with silence and to live at 'the still centre of the turning world'. The process of Zen meditation is rather different. A good analogy is that of the 'judo trip'. The skill in judo is to pull one's opponent in one direction until he is committed and then to trip him. His own momentum then throws him over. Similarly in Zen meditation the mind is used to take the consciousness in a particular direction and then, just as the mind is moving in a focused way, it is 'tripped' and surprised into a new experience. The idea then is not to stop all thought and to sit silently in meditation, but to use focused thought to break through into 'no-thought'. Then the eyes are opened and Zen is no longer a question of meditation but of walking, working, eating, of life. It is meditation without an object, meditation which takes place in life and not in the meditation hall. The focus is on the experience and not on the explanation. The outcome is not only mindfulness but the experience of reality as being 'the silence underlying sound, the Self in which the self is drowned'.[13]

It should not be thought, of course, that God is always to be found through silence. Archbishop Anthony Bloom, when opening a quiet day of silence for Anglican bishops attending the 1978 Lambeth Conference at Canterbury, told them,

I don't want to see you reading any holy books today. Reading a holy book is only just a way of escaping from boredom. It is much better if you are bored to read a newspaper or a paperback novel. At least then you are admitting to yourself that you are tired of just your company and God.

Listening is an art and listening to God is a very difficult art, especially in the late-twentieth-century Western world where we are all so impatient and often feel guilty if we think we are 'wasting time'. There is a nice story of a man who on retirement wanted to take up an absorbing hobby. A friend told him of an expert in collecting jade. 'Why don't you go to him and ask him to teach you?' he suggested. It seemed like a good idea and off the man went. At the start of the first session the expert gave him a piece of jade and told him to examine it closely. He then left him for half-an-hour, returned, took the jade away and asked for a fee of £10. The man was puzzled but returned for a second and third session, becoming increasingly irritated when the pattern was repeated: a piece of jade being put into his hand, then being left with it for half-an-hour, then a fee of £10 being charged. But he persevered. A few weeks later he met the friend who had first suggested that he learn about jade. 'How's it going?' his friend asked. 'Terrible', the disciple replied. 'The expert you suggested may know his stuff, but he doesn't teach me anything; he just leaves me by myself with a piece of jade for half-an-hour and then charges me £10. I wouldn't mind, but the piece he gave me to examine last time was a fake!'

Progress in meditation can be equally real but invisible and not necessarily for the impatient, as a poem by Edwina Gately indicates.

SILENT GOD

Silent God,
empty, sound-less,
like the long dark nights
without life,
I wait, gently hoping,
for your touch which says,
'I'm here.'
But the void remains,
Unfilled.
Silent God,
Why do you hide your face
from me?[14]

Listening and often not finding God as a desert monk, or on a self-chosen retreat away from everyday life, may be frustrating and even sometimes sad, but it is not the disaster it must be when God is silent in the face of danger, suffering and death.

It is one thing to choose silence and quite another to be thrust into a silent world unwillingly. It is when it is imposed upon an unwilling victim that silence may be a negative and even sometimes a destructive force rather than creative or spirit-filled. Prisoners who are kept in solitary confinement may be destroyed. Describing his time in a prison cell, when he was a hostage in the Middle East, Brian Keenan wrote of

the slow down-dragging slide and pull into hopeless depression and weariness. The waters of the sea of despair are heavy and thick and I think I cannot swim through them.[15]

Brian Keenan did somehow manage to swim through his despair and to rediscover his creativity and imagination, though sometimes even this was an escape from the hideous situation he was in to another world of madness and torture As time went on he relied more and more on his imagination, to relive the past or simply to enliven a dull day. In the middle of his captivity he had the courage to begin to write down some of his experiences and to write poems which sprang up into a life of their own, such as 'A bicycle designed in the cell'.

Elizabeth Barrett Browning was thrust into silence through grief at the age of 34, and the grief and the silence returned to her spasmodically throughout her life. In 1840 she was in Torquay convalescing, with her beloved brother to keep her company. Her father wished 'Bro' to return to London, but Elizabeth insisted that he should stay with her. It was a calm and sunny July day when he went sailing with some of his friends and did not return. Elizabeth later wrote about the agony of the three-day wait in the sunny weather, with the sea bright and smooth and taunting. She was ill for months, half-conscious and with a wandering mind, unable to write or express herself articulately. Twenty years later, in 1860, Elizabeth's sister Henrietta died and she returned to a state of helpless and despairing grief, unable to cry or speak. She wrote about her condition of grief as monotonous like the waves of the sea. She wrote of her fate of being able to write for the benefit of others, though her writing was of no consolation to herself. She did write poems about the death of her brother, and it seems that they were wrenched out of her unwilling dumbness. It seems that her creativity and inspiration came to her through her suffering silence almost against her will.

TEARS

> Thank God. Bless God, all ye who suffer not
> More grief than ye can weep for. That is well –
> That is light grieving! Lighter, none befell
> Since Adam forfeited the primal lot.
> Tears! What are tears? The babe weeps in its cot,
> The mother singing; at her marriage bell
> The bride weeps, and before the oracle
> Of high-faned hills the poet has forgot
> Such moisture on his cheeks. Thank God for grace,
> Ye who weep only! If, as some have done,
> Ye grope tear-blinded in a desert place
> And touch but tombs – look up! Those tears will run
> Soon in long rivers down the lifted face,
> And leave the vision clear for stars and sun.
>   Elizabeth Barrett Browning

The grace of God and consolation, it seemed to Elizabeth, were for those who could weep, and not for those who, like herself, could not. Minority groups often speak of the silence they feel surrounding them from societies where the majority population does not even notice their presence, let alone seek to listen and understand, and even less to weep with them.

The worst silence of all can seem to be the silence of the inner spirit, the silence emanating from weariness and from apparent emptiness. But paradoxically the silent emptiness of the spirit may be more likely to lead to new richness than the full-to-overflowing spirits of some who are very content with themselves. There is a Zen Buddhist story of Nan-in, the Japanese master during the Meiji era, who received a university professor who came to ask about Zen. Nan served the tea, and filled his visitor's cup and then continued to pour out the tea so that the cup overflowed. The professor said, in some agitation, 'The cup is overfull. No more will go in.' Nan then told the professor that he was like the cup, 'full of your own opinions and speculations. How can I show Zen unless you first empty your cup?'[16] An emptiness of spirit may sharply remind human beings of their weakness and need to listen, to God, to other human beings, and to their own revived inner spirit.

Westerners who are brought up to argue about everything, from what we eat and wear to politics and religion, find it hard to listen to God and even harder to listen to other people. Most of us enjoy a good argument, which is fine so long as there are times when we stop to listen to others. But sometimes we pretend to listen or think we are listening whilst always remaining quietly confident that our ways and wisdoms are best. Perhaps we would be on the way to listening to and respecting others if we could begin to admit that whilst we may believe that our own ways and wisdoms are best, certainly in our experience, other people of other cultures and faiths are also following what they believe to be best for them.

Charles de Foucauld, who died in 1916, was a desert hermit who followed in the footsteps of the earlier monks, spent most of his time in prayer and meditation, but does not seem to have had much appreciation of the desert people around him as they actually were, only as he desired to change them, towards France and towards Christianity. A Buddhist in the North of England told us that he had tried very hard to get to know some local Christians, but in the end he had given up because they had kept trying to persuade him to become a Christian whilst not being interested in his faith. Listening to others may lead to appreciation and understanding but only when there is openness and trust. We may have to struggle really to understand and value other people, especially those of other faiths and cultures.

Kahlil Gibran expressed this poetically:

OF TALKING

When you meet your friend on the roadside or
   in the market place, let the spirit in you move
   your lips and direct your tongue.
Let the voice within your voice speak to the ear
   of his ear;
For his soul will keep the truth of your heart
   as the taste of wine is remembered.
When the colour is forgotten and the vessel is
   no more.[17]

It is in the silence of the heart that the miracle of communication can effectively take place. There is a powerful Jewish story which illustrates this. When the great Rabbi Israel Baal Shem-Tov saw misfortune threatening his people, it was his custom to go into a certain part of the forest to meditate. There he would light a fire, say a special prayer, and the miracle would be accomplished and the misfortune averted.

Later, when his disciple the celebrated Magid of Mezritch had occasion, for the same reason, to intercede with heaven, he would go to the same place in the forest and say, 'Master of the Universe, listen! I do not know how to light the fire, but I am still able to say the prayer.' And, again, the miracle would be accomplished. Still later, Rabbi Moshe-Leib of Sasov, in order to save his people once more, would go into the forest and say, 'I do not know how to light the fire. I do not know the prayer, but I know the place and this must be sufficient.'

Then it fell to Rabbi Israel of Rizhyn to overcome misfortune. Sitting in his armchair, his head in his hands, he spoke to God, 'I am unable to light the fire and I do not know the prayer. I cannot even find the place in the forest. All I can do is to tell the story, and this must be sufficient.' And it was sufficient.[18]

Saint in the desert, worshipper in an empty church, elderly person confined to an armchair in the living room – the story of faith in the silence of the heart is sufficient.

NOTES

1. D. Adams, *Fire of the North – the Illustrated Life of St Cuthbert* (SPCK, London, 1993).
2. A. Wainwright, *Fellwalking with Wainwright* (Michael Joseph, London, 1984).
3. 'Best Society', in *Philip Larkin – Collected Poems*, ed. A. Thwaite (Marvell Press and Faber and Faber, London, 1988).
4. J. Rule, *Desert of the Heart* (Pandora Press, London, 1990).
5. Sri Aurobindo, *Collected Poems* (Sri Aurobindo Society, India, 1964).
6. Chandogya Upanishad, *The Upanishads*, trans. Juan Mascaro (Penguin Classics, London, 1965).
7. C. G. Jung, *Man and His Symbols* (Arkana, London, 1990).
8. J. Hopewell, 'Jyoti Sahi – An Indian Approach to Christian Art' *Church Times*, 3 February 1995.
9. Maitri Upanishad, *The Upanishads*, trans. Juan Mascaro (Penguin Classics, London, 1965).

10. *Bhagavad Gita – the Gospel of the Lord Shri Krishna*, trans. Shsri Purohit Swami (Faber and Faber, London, 1978), chapter 6.

11. C. Lawson, talk at Woodbrooke College.

12. A Carthusian, *They Speak by Silences* (Longmans, Green, London, 1955).

13. C. Humphreys, *The Search Within* (Sheldon Press, London, 1977).

14. E. Gately, *I Hear a Seed Growing* (Anthony Clark, Wheathampstead, Herts, 1990).

15. B. Keenan, *An Evil Cradling* (Hutchinson, London, 1992).

16. G. Zukav, *The Dancing Wu Li Masters – an Overview of the New Physics* (Bantam, London, 1979).

17. K. Gibran, *The Prophet* (Heinemann, London, 1965).

18. S. Kopp, *If You Meet the Buddha on the Road, Kill Him!* (Sheldon Press, London, 1974).

CHAPTER SIX

Sacred Worship

IN CHAPTER THREE we described the African experience of 'tuning in' to the beat of the universe – 'In the beginning was the beat' is at the heart of African spirituality. In the rhythm of the dance, men and women resonate with the heartbeat of the universe and then 'impose' their own rhythm upon it, so that the powerful beat of life begins to work for them in hunting, war, love, healing or the other life-important needs and experiences.

This is no bad approach to a more general understanding of worship – worship as a sacred dance before God, resonating and engaging with the life of God, and through so doing having access to divine grace and power. When we first visited Hong Kong we were surprised to find the local parks crowded early in the morning with people, young and old, engaged in the Chinese traditional spiritual dance of the T'ai Chi Ch'uan. The stylized movements combine physical and mental discipline and detachment. As the practitioner's limbs move through the motions of the dance, his or her flow of thought is concentrated upon the meaning behind the movement – the dance of heaven engaging with the dance of life.

The dance of Siva from the Hindu tradition is similarly a dance which links God to the earth. In the traditional portrayal, one of Siva's hands points downwards in commitment, whilst another is outstretched in blessing. One foot stands on and crushes a creature representing evil, whilst the other is raised, as the lord of the dance is poised between earth and heaven. He dances the cosmos into and out of existence within a fiery arch of flames denoting consciousness.

In the Old Testament we are told that the great King David,

who centralized Jewish worship by building the first temple at Jerusalem, danced before the ark of the Lord in ecstasy (2 Sam 6.14). There are forms of worship today which exhibit equal excitement and lack of inhibition – the tradition of the whirling dervishes in Islam, the powerful soul singing and participatory preaching in some black-led churches in the US and Britain, the singing, dancing, 'speaking in tongues', and 'slaying in the spirit' of the fervent Christian charismatic congregation. Few of these experiences are the spontaneous 'dancing before the lord' of King David. Like the African dance, most have their own form, content and pattern – even within the most free 'shared prayer' part of a Christian charismatic service there will be an expectation about what form, language, style and length is appropriate worship for this particular congregation.

And to go to the other extreme, in the Quaker meeting there is in theory no set pattern, and any Friend is encouraged to share, if he or she wishes, words of the spirit. Such a meeting, however, has its ways of discouraging a 'noisy' Friend who contributes too frequently and at too great length, or of encouraging an over-'quiet' group of Friends to be a little more vocal.

The singing of songs and choruses is to be found as an element in the worship of many mainline Christian churches, particularly at family or youth services, and liturgical dance groups are also a feature of modern church life. On the other hand, many churches have learned from the Friends the value of a time of silence within worship and it is not unusual for a time of intercession to be preceded, and Bible readings to be followed, by such a period of silence.

There are those who may feel that 'ordinary' church worshippers are not able to handle silence. If so they may be surprised to attend one of the ordinary services at the Taizé community, where, as we have described in an earlier chapter, within the round of three services a day there is ten minutes of profound silence. To sit in the midst of a sea of young Christians as they meditate in silence is both awesome and uplifting, and certainly refutes those who would claim that such serious discipline is beyond the scope of ordinary church folk.

Taizé is not, however, best noted for its silence within worship. It is better known for the creative way in which the community uses moving music and profound words which are accessible to the most casual pilgrim. It is not perhaps a coincidence that the symbol of Taizé is the 'dancing cross' which appeared in the 1960s and 1970s, during the era of youth 'flower power', peace and justice, long hair, bells and guitars, as a large brass medallion, the size of a horse-brass, circular in shape, with a hollow dancing cross at the heart. Gradually that large, crude, hollow dancing cross has been replaced by the cross itself, at first equally large and made of the same material – brass. But over the years the cross has become smaller and it is now made of fine enamel or porcelain so as to blend in with the more sophisticated youth fashions of the nineties. But it is still recognizably the dancing cross, which still appropriately illustrates the life and worship of a community that has managed to continue to be relevant to successive changes in youth culture.

It is creative to compare the sign of the dancing cross within the context of Christian liturgy with the African traditional dance. There are similarities and differences. In Christian worship, through word and music, the congregation 'tunes in' to the divine life, and in penitence opens up its life to the forgiving life of heaven. This life is clarified and expounded upon through the biblical readings and sermon. The congregation affirms its commitment to the beat of the heart of God in credal affirmations, and then comes a time of intercessory prayer, which for many is the most profound part of the service.

And here the dance of Christian liturgy begins to depart from that of traditional African dance. In African culture we have suggested that, having tuned into the beat of the universe, the dancing tribe imposes its beat upon it, to make the power of the universe work for it. There is no suggestion in Christian intercession of the worshipping congregation attempting to impose its will upon God, although it is not unknown for those leading prayer to attempt to steer God in the way that the leader feels he should go; neither is it unknown for individuals to enter in plea-bargaining with God: 'Do this for me, God, and I'll do this for you.' But in general this is not in the spirit of Christian prayer, which takes the form of tuning into the divine life through penitence and absolution, deepening awareness of the divine through biblical and homiletic word, and then the liturgical dance moving on to the congregation sharing with a gracious God its concerns for a wounded and suffering world –

not to dictate to, manipulate, or even plead with God to act, because the power of the God whom Christians know through Jesus has been shown through the mysterious weakness of the cross. Indeed, if the dance of liturgy is a Eucharist then this mystery will be shown explicitly through bread broken, wine poured out, 'Christ's body broken, Christ's blood shed'.

There are four actions within the 'dance' of the eucharistic prayer. The bread and wine are taken, offered to God in blessing, broken, and given. Through these actions the worshipping community is linked with the historical sacrifice of Jesus who, during the agony in the Garden of Gethsemane following the Last Supper, took up his life and offered it to his heavenly Father: 'nevertheless not my will but yours be done' (Luke 22). The next day that body was broken and his blood poured out on the cross. Yet through the miracle of the cross/resurrection, that body became a gift of new life when it was encountered and received, first by the apostles and then through worship and prayer by all Christians everywhere.

The eucharistic elements, bread broken, wine poured out, are thus living sacraments of the fourfold action of the historical Jesus, taking, blessing, breaking and giving, but they are also symbols of the life of the congregation gathered in worship. It is the life of the congregation linked to the life of Jesus Christ through the words and actions of the eucharistic prayer which is touched, taken, blessed, broken and then given by God as a gift to the world. Corporate worship is not the same as a group of individuals gathered to pray together in the same place. In the eucharistic rite of the Church of England *Alternative Service Book* the president of the Eucharist reminds the congregation, before the eucharistic prayer commences, of 'who they are'. 'We are the Body of Christ. In the one Spirit we were all baptized into one body. Let us then pursue all that makes for peace and builds up our common life.'[1]

The bread and wine represent that common life. The liturgy of the Church of South India reminds participants of the scattered seed which went into the earth to make the grain for their bread. 'As this bread was once scattered seed, O Bread of life, sown in the earth to die and rise to new life, so gather all peoples together in one humanity of your coming new age.' When grain is made into bread it has to be ground down so that the individual grains merge and lose their distinctiveness in the flour. The flour in turn loses its distinctiveness as it is mixed with yeast and water, and what emerges is the new loaf. The new loaf has a unity which is greater than the sum of its former parts, unlike a plate of cooked rice. So the eucharistic bread represents the total life of the congregation gathered to dedicate themselves as the Body of Christ in their locality, to be taken, blessed, broken and given, whilst the blood of their commitment, following the example of Jesus Christ on the cross, is poured out for the glory of God and the good of his world. The liturgy of the Church of South India takes up this breaking and giving in the 'Bread Prayer':

As this bread is broken and this wine poured out, O Seeker and Saviour of the lost, we remember again the poor and oppressed of the earth. We recall that your body was broken that the hungry might be nourished, the oppressed set free, replenished with the bread of new hope and new life.[2]

The cross, not the drum, then, is the sign of Christian worship, because the divine power which the worshipper is tuning into and empathizing with is the power which shows itself in weakness – the weakness of the cross. And yet, appropriately, in Taizé this is a dancing cross, because the weakness and pain of the cross were followed by the unexpected miracle of the resurrection and the new life of church and world. Jyoti Sahi often represents Christ on the cross as a dancer, bringing suffering and hope together in one image. The cross itself can helpfully be seen as a dancing cross, because in worship we tune in to a God who shows his power and strength not only in the weakness of the cross, but in the unexpected happening of the resurrection which led humanity on a new dance of life, hope and vigour. The authentic style of Christian community living can be seen as that dancing cross, therefore, and the dancing cross can be seen as the style of authentic Christian worship.

In 'Dinkaland' in the Sudan an impressive new church is built in the form of a cross where the people gather for the dance of worship. A recent visitor recorded,

The church is the largest and most impressive building of local construction I've seen in the Sudan, the labour of thousands of committed souls. Beautifully thatched, it rises to perhaps thirty feet at its centre. Amidst a forest of supporting poles, like a primitive cathedral, the congregation (numbering some four thousand on our visit) fills the arms of the cross, all facing towards a central dais.[3]

Nowhere do people more need the grace-filled power of the cross, linked to both suffering and glory, than in the Sudan where Bishop Nathaniel Garong works constantly to encourage his people by assuring them that 'God has not discarded you'.

They would have been encouraged had they experienced another unexpected dance celebrating new life in Africa which took place in St Martin-in-the-Fields Church in Trafalgar Square. Following a service in remembrance of those who died as victims of injustice and violence in South Africa, Bishop Desmond Tutu unveiled a bronze sculpture by Chaim Stephenson portraying a dead Soweto child being carried by a gaunt father, and then, led by Desmond Tutu, people danced up the aisles towards the open doors and out into a new life of hope.

All too often worship in the faith traditions does not dance. Ordinary life, through worship, should be touched by the holy so that the worshipper can return to ordinary life inspired and challenged. This does not always happen, for good reasons. The dynamic of worship can be compared to the dynamic of one kind of coffee percolator. This type of percolator has a basket of ground coffee suspended above a pot of water. Heat is applied and the water warms up, and as it does, it rises up a central tube and then drops back through the ground coffee, taking on its flavour. After several such cycles the water has become rich coffee which can then be poured out and used. The dynamic of worship can be seen in a similar way. The worshippers, like the water in the pot, come in perhaps feeling insipid, lukewarm, weakened by the stresses and strains of everyday living. Through religious words, music and rituals, the heat of worship warms the heart and lifts the soul, which rises to touch the sense of the numinous, awe, wonder – divine forgiveness and challenge. Then the worshipper is sent out strengthened and enriched, to be poured out once more in a life of witness and service.

Things can go wrong with this dynamic which deprives it of authenticity. Returning to the analogy of the coffee-pot, it is possible to imagine some problems. One might forget to apply the heat to the pot. If so, no matter how full the pot might be of water, no matter how fine the quality of the ground coffee, all that will come out of the pot is tepid water. Equally, worship can be lukewarm and uninspiring, so that hearts and souls are not uplifted, the sense of the holy is not encountered and worshippers emerge without the sense of being forgiven and challenged. Formal worship might have occurred but it has had no effect upon the lives of the worshippers. All too often acts of worship at school can be like this, and if so it is little wonder that children grow up believing that worship is boring and empty. It then takes an experience of worship of real power, such as that at Taizé, to move any person to pray and praise. Once inspiring worship is experienced, however, there is a 'divine dissatisfaction' with any watered-down, merely formal, imitations.

Another way in which the dynamic of worship may get distorted can be illustrated by a coffee-pot full of water but with no ground coffee in the basket. Heat might well be applied, the hot water will circulate, but all that will emerge is hot water, because there is no coffee to enrich it. In the case of worship this is analogous to the community where there is a great deal of warmth and companionship but little sense of the holy or numinous. People may well be encouraged and helped by community life and ritual but it is doubtful whether such rituals, devoid of the sense of the divine, can be described as worship or have the effect of people taking a sense of the holy with them into their everyday lives.

The polar opposite of this is the coffee-pot in which the ground coffee is included, heat is applied, but little or no water is put into the pot. After a while there will be a distinctive and rather unpleasant smell, but any coffee which is eventually produced will be virtually undrinkable. The same can be true of churches, temples or sects where there may be intense and vibrant worship, but where the worshippers are cut off from the community and perhaps obsessed with holy actions, rituals and words. The ordinary life of such worshippers is likely to seem 'churchy', fanatical, narrow-minded and unattractive. In fact there is little space for ordinary life, because most time is spent in or around the church, or on church matters.

A parable of powerful ritual losing touch with reality is to be found in the chilling opening chapters of William Golding's *The Lord of the Flies*.[4] A party of schoolboys are wrecked on an island. They have the sense to realize that if they are to be rescued it is vital for them to keep a signal fire going night and day, and feeding the fire becomes an important part of the round of daily living. It is a practical task but it also reminds them of their connection with a wider world, and holds their hopes for the future. Soon, however, other more primitive rituals take over. The members of the group who had been in a choir march solemnly along the beach in their robes. They become a dominant group for whom the rituals of disciplined music are transformed into the rituals of the hunt – with the prey changing ultimately from being animal to being human. Most of the other boys are caught up into this excitement. Meanwhile the feeding of the fire, their connection with wider community and future hope, is gradually forgotten or ignored, and the fire eventually goes out.

Feeding the fire of worship with rich and symbolic words and actions equally connects the worshipping congregation with a wider faith-community, in both time and space, and holds their hope for the future of themselves, their community and their planet. The quiet though deep encounter with the holy in such worship is enriching and sustaining. Like the choir on the beach, however, it can be lost in the ritual of empty forms which, though perhaps touching and triggering deep emotions, can become an end in themselves – time-consuming, engrossing, compulsive. Ultimately when this happens the wider reality is forgotten and the fire of the holy goes out.

Sometimes rituals which are empty or oppressive can only be ended or changed by dramatic happenings. A story from the Pacific Islands tells of a particular tribe who had a sacred ritual which they held on the shortest day of the year. The origin of the ritual lay in the mists of time but obviously stemmed from the fact that the days were becoming shorter and shorter. The tribe interpreted this as the sun, the source of their heat, light and life, departing from them. To change the sun's mind and cause it to return to them, the whole tribe gathered on the beach at dawn, a young warrior dressed in a sacred robe knelt before them, and the priest of the tribe struck off his head with the sacred sword. Through this sacrifice, it was thought, the sun god was placated and returned to give the tribe light and life for another year.

The time came when the priest of the tribe reached the age when he felt it right to hand on his sacred duties to his son. His son was not convinced of the necessity of the yearly sacrifice and asked his father what evidence there was that the sacrifice was linked to the return of the sun. The old priest scolded his son for asking such sacrilegious questions. His father before him, and his before him had been content to do their priestly duty and so must his son. Nothing his son said could persuade him otherwise, so in the end the boy asked his father if at least he could select the victim. The father agreed and told the boy to be there on the beach at dawn the next morning with the young man who would be sacrificed.

Dawn came and the victim, dressed in the sacred robe, head covered with a hood, knelt on the beach, but the priest's son was nowhere to be seen. The ceremony could not be delayed, however, and the priest, whilst saying the correct prayers and performing the correct movements, struck off the head of the victim. It was only then he discovered that the victim was his own son. The boy had sacrificed himself in the hope that this would bring priest and people to a new outlook. There were no more unthinking sacrifices made by that tribe, and the sun continued to rise.

The Old Testament prophets repeatedly emphasized that there must be a connection between worship and life. Empty sacrifices accompanied by godless living are worthless. The most explicit was Amos, who has God saying,

I hate, I despise your feasts, and I take no delight in your solemn assemblies. Even though you offer me your burnt offerings and cereal offerings, I will not accept them ... Take away from me the noise of your songs; to the melody of your harps I will not listen. But let justice roll down like waters, and righteousness like an ever-flowing stream.

(Amos 5.21–24)

Jesus of Nazareth taught in the tradition of these prophets and indeed challenged the formal worship of his people at its very heart in the temple at Jerusalem. That challenge was certainly one of the elements which brought him to his death, and it is not difficult to make connections between the story of his teaching and death and the story of the boy on the Pacific beach.

The dynamic of worship going askew in a false connection between the secular and the sacred is often to be found in folk or popular religion. The belief is that proper religious actions automatically result in desirable consequences in life, and therefore it is worth paying in terms of money or time for the protection of a kind of 'divine good luck'. It is fascinating to wander around a Tao temple in Hong Kong, for example, and see people spending money for sticks to be thrown, through which the experts claim to forecast the future. And you don't have to go to Hong Kong to see this. Plenty of people in our society today supplement their income by preying on fears or hopes, particularly those of young people, and claim to predict the future through the use of Tarot cards and other magical means.

But magic and worship are not the same thing. They may both make a connection with the archetypal deeps of the human psyche, but magic claims an automatic cause and effect. 'Do this, say that, and the result will be this.' Worship is something quite different. It uses the awe and wonder of religious ritual to experience a sense of the holy. And the great faith-traditions emphasize that, unlike magic, the sense of the holy is not a sense of divine creepiness; the holy shows itself in the experience of forgiveness, acceptance, wonder, challenge, and self-sacrifice. True worship has a connection with life, but it is not the mechanical connection of magic, it is the connection made through the changed and enriched lives of the worshippers who take the divine into the ordinary through costly living.

To be fair, however, those who indulge in personal magic often have a sense of concern for others. For example, in the same temples in Hong Kong where people are throwing magical sticks, you can see worshippers making sacrifices of paper cars, suitcases, houses, and money so that a deceased relative is fully supplied with all necessities on the journey past death. In a country like Japan where several religions are to be found existing side by side on a 'live and let live' basis, folk religion takes on a very pragmatic approach. The men or women in the street seem to take their newborn babies to the Shinto shrine for blessing, their marriages to the Christian church, and their deaths to the Buddhist temple.

We happened to visit a major Shinto shrine at Kamakura shortly after the prior of the temple had returned from a global peace-gathering sponsored by the Pope for religious leaders at Assisi. The prior was very indignant that he had not been allowed to receive communion at the Roman Catholic mass which had been held, whereas, he pointed out to us, we were welcome to participate fully in the whole life of his shrine. He cheered up considerably when we told him that we as Anglicans would also not be allowed to receive communion at a Roman Catholic mass.

When Ronald Eyre on his *Long Search*[5] visited Japan he was fascinated by the Buddhist traditions and teachings. In particular he was intrigued by the dialogue between the two religious concepts contained in the Japanese words *jiriki* and *tariki*, *jiriki* meaning 'self-help' and *tariki* meaning 'waiting on the help of another'. The question is, 'What is the nature of the spiritual power that is available to mould my life?' Is it a power within myself to be sought, touched, harnessed and employed through spiritual disciplines? Or is it a power beyond and outside myself which I am powerless to control or obstruct and to which I merely offer up myself in worship? Do I take action and have life, or do I take no action and have life more abundantly? These are questions which go to the heart of spirituality in all traditions and all faiths, of course. In Christian terms words such as 'grace' and 'providence' hold the reality of God's initiative and freedom, whilst the disciplines of intercessory prayer and meditation hold the experience that the spiritual pilgrim must work hard, or at least consciously co-operate in making spiritual progress.

A parable of trustful acceptance encountering direct action comes from an unlikely source, James Clavell's epic novel *Shogun*, set in sixteenth-century Japan.[6] Late one night when the weather was appalling, a report was received that a ship had been wrecked on a dangerous part of the coast. A party of soldiers was sent out to investigate and bring back any survivors. After a difficult march they reached the top of the cliffs surrounding the bay where the reports had located the shipwreck, and they saw that not only was there the wreckage of a ship but at least one sailor was lying unconscious on the beach.

One of the soldiers came to his captain and said, 'I was brought up in a mountainous region of our country where we climbed for pleasure and pride. Let me try to climb down the cliff and attempt to rescue the sailor.' The captain gave his permission and the climber started down, but even his skill was not sufficient to master the sheer cliff and when he was almost down he slipped and fell heavily. As he landed he felt a searing pain shooting up his leg, but being a man of discipline he told himself, 'I will feel no pain', and he walked stiffly across to the body by the water. He was delighted to find that the sailor, though unconscious, was still alive. He turned to shout the good news to his comrades on the cliff top. It was only then that he noticed that they were shouting and waving at him. It took him a little while to realize that they were warning him that the tide was coming in rapidly and that he was already in danger.

He searched every way for a means of escape but there was none: the bay was cut off by the waves and the cliffs were too sheer to be climbed even by a fit man. And certainly a man with a twisted ankle stood no chance. There was no escape and so he turned to face the sea, sat down on a rock and composed himself for inevitable death, saying to himself, 'What a wonderful last day, how beautiful the last sky, last sea, last light. What a joy to have time to meditate'. And so he sank into a deep meditative trance.

Meanwhile his comrades on the cliff top were frantically trying to find a way of rescuing their friend. They searched the cliff for caves or ledges which would give him sanctuary. Finally their captain spotted a thin scar on the cliff face, invisible from below but wide enough to support a man. The soldiers shouted in triumph to their comrade, but deep in his meditative trance, he was deaf to their cries. They picked up rocks and threw them down to attract his attention, but all to no avail.

Finally the captain rose, bowed gravely to his men, then with a horrific cry threw himself over the cliff. He landed at the feet of the doomed man. The shout and the crash jerked the soldier out of his trance and he whirled around, listened to the instructions from above and scrambled on to the ledge with his still-unconscious load. They were saved, but at the cost of the life of their captain.

This story could be a parable of several faith-traditions, and illustrates well the dynamic between the Japanese Buddhist notions of *jiriki*, 'self-help', and *tariki*, 'waiting on the help of another'. In the sacrifice of the captain for the salvation of his soldier lies the echo of the story of Buddhist saints who, on the edge of entering nirvana themselves, turn back to the world for the sake of helping their comrades along the spiritual road to bliss.

Christians can also see echoes of their own faith-story in this parable. It is not difficult to read the gospel story as that of Jesus Christ sacrificing himself to wake up and rescue a world that was sunk deep into a trance of habit, sin, selfishness and piety. The shock of the death of their leader on the cross had the effect of jerking his followers out of their trance, and they became resurrected people, escaping with him from the grip of sin and death and spreading around the world in the power of his Holy Spirit with the good news of new life.

In effective worship, we encounter once more that shocking, living word of God, which wakes us up from our taken-for-granted daily life and predictable, comfortable piety; and being awakened, we have the opportunity of living costly lives with and for God and for the people of the world to whom he would bring 'life in abundance'. Through such understanding our worship and world can 'dance'.

A prayer at the end of the *Alternative Service Book* service of Holy Communion expresses this understanding:

Father of all, we give you thanks and praise, that when we were still far off you met us in your Son and brought us home. Dying and living, he declared your love, gave us grace, and opened the gate of glory. May we who share Christ's body live his risen life; we who drink his cup bring life to others; we whom the Spirit lights give light to the world. Keep us firm in the hope you have set before us, so we and all your children shall be free, and the whole earth live to praise your name; through Christ our Lord. Amen.[7]

NOTES

1. *The Alternative Service Book 1980* (Oxford University Press).
2. *The Church of South India Liturgy. The Holy Eucharist* (The Christian Literature Society, Madras, 1985).
3. Marc Nikkel, letter to CMS, June 1994.
4. W. Golding, *Lord of the Flies* (Faber and Faber, London, 1954).
5. R. Eyre, *The Long Search* (Fount, London, 1979).
6. J. Clavell, *Shogun* (Hodder and Stoughton, London, 1975).
7. *The Alternative Service Book 1980* (Oxford University Press).

CHAPTER SEVEN

Sacred Community

WE HAVE a gift from Kenya in our drawing-room. It is a Makonde 'people pile' and it is beautifully carved and polished. The people of the African community are all on top of each other and their faces show expressions of joy, sorrow, peace and pain. It is interesting to reflect whether they are there in love, to support each other in happiness and trouble and in shared work; or whether they are exploiting each other or crushing each other into a prison-house of conformity and misery, with no particular aim except perhaps that of survival. Both views may well be true, of the different people in the pile, or even of the same people at different times and in different circumstances. What is certainly true is the fact that human beings are made to live in community. Individuals are both moulded by community and help to mould it, and the same is true for individual believers and faith-communities.

The most basic and universal form of human community is the family. Whether nuclear or extended, it is within the family that children grow in security, receive an understanding of themselves and their culture, and are challenged to develop their strengths and moderate their weaknesses in the service of others. The same elements are to be found within faith-communities where the teaching and rituals in the family are a vital ingredient in the developing spirituality of the family members.

In Judaism, if the synagogue is the place where the faith is further expounded and taught and where worship and prayer are offered, such teaching and prayer are built upon the foundations laid in Jewish family life, where every member of the family is valued and honoured and has a part to play in the religious life of the home. Every week the Sabbath is welcomed in the home by the woman of the house lighting at least two candles, with daughters lighting others. Before eating the Sabbath meal a ceremony called kiddush is performed, which involves drinking wine and blessing the day. Then the man of the house praises his wife, and the children are blessed. And so the meal progresses with the blessing of bread and the singing of Sabbath songs, ending with a thanksgiving. Whilst the main event of the Sabbath will be attendance at a service in the synagogue, the day will mostly be spent as a family day where ordinary duties are put aside. The end of the Sabbath is marked in the home by wine being poured over the candle to put it out and everybody present wishing each other a good week.

If this is the weekly pattern, the year is also marked by religious festivals, many of which have their family rituals. The festival of Passover marking the escape of the Jewish people from slavery in Egypt, for example, is preceded by a thorough cleaning of the home to remove every crumb of old food. The most popular part of the festival is the home celebration of the Seder meal during which the Haggadah is read, telling the story of the Exodus in a vivid and imaginative way. New generations, therefore, become thoroughly familiar with this basic faith-story, and to press home the teaching the youngest child present will ask the Four Questions from the Haggadah which begin, 'Why is this night so different from all other nights?' The child will not only be answered in words but in actions, because each course of the meal and every food eaten has a significance which is further explained: the roast lamb representing the Passover lamb slain in Egypt; the bitter herbs a symbol of the bitter life of slavery; the mixture of chopped apple, nuts, cinnamon and wine, a symbol of the mortar used by the Jewish slaves to make bricks; the dish of salt water, representing the tears shed during the long years in captivity. In this way, then, the Jewish family members not only strengthen their own bonds, one with another, but they strengthen the bonds of faith which link them to their religious roots and connect them with their world-wide Jewish community, and they pass on their faith to a new generation of believers.

From this sense of family community, to be found in all the world faiths, a wider sense of community is developed. In Islam the *umma*, the worldwide community of the faithful, brings

Muslims together through the law of God which both confers privileges on them and requires duties of them. The *umma* can be small, comprising two or more persons, or can be as large as a society. It can then be local, national or global. In August 1990 Muslim organizations meeting at the Islamic Cultural Centre in London to discuss the developing crisis in the Gulf issued a declaration insisting that 'current national borders ... are artificial divisions. The nation of Islam (*umma*) is one ... and national borders cannot be more sacred than the security of Muslim blood and land.'[1] The *umma*, then, is of the essence of Islamic self-understanding and self-confidence, for Muslims see themselves first and foremost as standing together, shoulder to shoulder, in *umma*, in worship and in service.

A member of the Sikh faith would well understand, because it is impossible to be a Sikh in isolation; community is absolutely necessary. Guru Nanak was born in 1469 and founded Sikhism. He always taught that the way people behaved to each other was far more important than their status in the community. One story tells of how Guru Nanak accepted an invitation to eat a meal with a poor man called Lalo. He had also been invited to dinner by a rich man called Malik Bhago, who was then angry because the Guru had chosen to eat with Lalo. Later, the Guru did go to Malik's house, taking with him some bread from Lalo's house. It seems that when he squeezed this bread it produced milk, whilst when he squeezed Malik's bread it produced blood – the blood of the people Malik had exploited in growing rich.

Nine Gurus followed Guru Nanak before the Sikh scriptures, which were named 'Guru Granth Sahib', became the permanent guide or guru. They are now read in the gurdwara by any Sikh man or woman, emphasizing the equality and the solidarity of the Sikh community. And if this sense of community is shown within the gurdwara in devotion it is also to be found just out-side. The third Guru, Amar Das, founded the *langar*, the open kitchen where anyone could eat. Today the Sikh community all over the world is still noted for its hospitality and service. 'Just as the castor oil plant imbibes the scent so the fallen become emancipated through the company of the faithful.'[2]

Many Sikhs come to a stage in their lives when they wish to join the *khalsa*, the community of those who have committed themselves to a devout Sikh religious path. The *khalsa* were originally those who resisted persecution and later built up a homeland for themselves in the Punjab. The division of the Punjab, with the partition of India and Pakistan in 1947, was a great sadness for Sikhs and many moved to other countries, including Britain. Sikhs are today divided, sometimes bitterly, between those who wish to struggle for a Sikh state (such people often wear orange turbans) and those who do not.

At their best, then, the communities of the world faiths give a coherent and secure environment within which the faith of a follower can deepen and broaden whilst being orientated also to the wider human community. Religious faith-communities, in giving such attention to the strengthening and nurturing of family life within the life of faith, are typical of most traditional faith-communities and societies. In such societies there is a great sense of interconnectedness. Every person has a place, no one is left out. Of course, within traditional societies living a fragile existence, a community could not afford to have disconnected 'maverick' individuals with no place or stake in the community. Strict rules emerged regarding marriage, for example, and in cases where there was a disproportion of males and females polygamy developed within the extended family so that no free-floating adults were available to threaten the stability and unity of the community. The traditional extended family has many attractions. The elderly have an honoured place and pass on their wisdom to new generations – no isolated old people's homes here. Children have the security of being cared for and disciplined by uncles and aunts in addition to their own parents, and grow up surrounded by a number of 'brothers' and 'sisters'. This is not to say that the child does not know exactly who everybody is. When we lived in Zambia the formula for introducing a cousin was, 'This is my brother (or sister),' whilst the words used when a 'real' brother or sister was introduced were, 'This is my brother (or sister) – one father, one mother.'

Some people when separated from their family feel a total loss of identity and suffer silently and miserably or may be so crushed that they do not fight for survival at all. They may sit down and despair, like the boy in the English boarding-school who felt so cut off from home and alienated from his new companions and school community that he slashed his wrists. Sometimes, however, the loss takes surprising forms and people are ashamed to admit, even to themselves, that they feel a sense of liberation. A priest told us of a woman he was helping whose husband had died. Six months later she crashed her car and her first feeling was one of relief that her husband would not be there when she went home to complain at the damage she had caused and ridicule her for her lack of driving skill. She had the self-honesty to admit that the death of her husband had not been all loss!

For many people the workplace is a 'second home' and provides a second family. It is a place where young men and women meet adults other than their parents, are influenced by them and learn not only new skills but the way in which people behave in adult society. It is not only destructive to the young man or woman, therefore, if no work can be found, but society is weakened because a generation grows up without the skills and disciplines which glue a community together. The experience can be equally destructive if a person is suddenly made redundant. It is not surprising that the shock can take the form of humiliation or denial and we read of men who dare not tell their wives that they are redundant, but who go through the pretence of going to work every day, only to sit in the local park.

The community of the workplace as an 'alternative' family, which emerges naturally as traditional societies encounter the challenges and problems of urban living, has been followed by a further development in community life, that of the base community made up, not of members of a natural human family, but of a family-sized unit of people sharing a common faith-commitment.

These base communities began to emerge in the 1960s within the slums and townships of the great cities of the world where traditional community life had fractured and failed, leaving people feeling powerless and alienated. In *The Community Called Church*,[3] J. L. Segundo gives the spiritual rationale for such communities. Christians know that they have been created to co-operate with the grace of God in loving their neighbour as themselves and they are stuck with that knowledge. And for the slum-dweller in Latin America to love neighbour as self is to get together with fellow Christians in Bible study and then not only to tackle individual sins, but to organize towards challenging and changing the sins of society. And because many powerful people have a vested interest in keeping society just the way it is, these base communities can expect opposition and suffering – so they know their need to stay close to one another and to God.

Rio Maria tells the story of life in Brazil's south-east Amazon region, where the rain forests are cut down and burnt and the wealthy ranchers and military police dominate life. It took the murder of Expedito Ribeiro de Souza, a trade unionist and poet, for the local people to unite to bring change. They looked to the Church for help. As one of the peasant farmers told his priest, 'The Church has to be like the seed of an orange, spread throughout the fruit, and entering into every segment. So when we are persecuted, the Church gives help, not betrayal.'[4]

'See, Judge, Act, Celebrate' is the dynamic of the base community. See what is going on in your corner of the world. Stay close to the people, listen to their stories, share their lives. Judge what are the fundamental issues, the deep currents beneath the waves of events. Judge what the Bible has to say about all this. Then act in the way that will be most effective. Act when the time is right. The most appropriate action comes as a miracle to people, changing their mind-set, changing their understanding of what is possible, giving them the courage to face the future with new hope and confidence. So finally, celebrate that new life and hope, before repeating the process.

The concept of the base community is not restricted to the cities of South America. In Britain the Archbishop's Commission for Urban Priority Areas in its report *Faith in the City*, published in 1985, placed great emphasis on the urban church and community being renewed through the action of 'local, outward-looking, and participating groups'. The creation of the Church Urban Fund has provided significant new resources for such inner-city faith-communities, and a wealth of local projects – housing, youth training, child care, job creation, urban forms of worship and mission – have come into existence.[5]

Many of these have involved co-operation between congregations of different Christian denominations. This partnership of faith has been extended through the creation of the Inner Cities Religious Council, whose members come from all the major world faiths represented in Britain's inner cities, whose chairman is the minister responsible for inner cities at the

Department of the Environment, and whose secretariat is
funded by both government and the faith communities. The
Council provides a central forum for sensitive issues such as
religious discrimination and youth unemployment in minority
faith-communities, and in its regional gatherings provides a
catalyst for the creation or strengthening of local councils of
faiths. What has become abundantly clear through this UK
experience is that, although urban religious communities of all
faiths feel themselves to be weak and fragile, they are very often
the strongest communities to be found in the inner cities, and
can form an effective basis for community regeneration.

This fact was appreciated some years ago by Saul Alinsky in
Chicago and formed the basis for the somewhat controversial
method of urban community regeneration called 'Broad-Based
Community Organizing'. Alinsky has striven to find ways of
'Seeing, Judging, Acting, and Celebrating' which are appropriate
to the inhabitants of the slums of US cities. The method is simple.
Add all the members of the congregations of Harlem or Brooklyn
or up-town Chicago together and you have a substantial number
of people – tens of thousands. Develop trained and disciplined
leaders from amongst them; focus on particular pressing issues;
determine the desired solutions; place these politely but firmly
before those having power or influence – politicians, corporate
heads and the like; then, if they do not listen, bring the people
out in a massive, though orderly and law-abiding, demonstration.

A story which gives a feel of the methods stems from the time
of the election of a mayor of New York. When running for office
the candidate had met with several of the base community
leaders and had agreed that, if he were elected, he would attend
a large meeting of local people to listen to the issues which they
wanted to raise with him. He was elected and he did attend the
meeting. The problem was, he refused to listen. On arrival he
told the organizers that he first wanted to deliver a forty-minute
speech, then the people could ask him questions. The organizers
politely told him that this was not the agreement he had made
with them; the people had had several earlier meetings and had
formulated the issues they wanted him to hear, they did not
want to listen to a politician giving a speech. At that the mayor
stormed out, unwisely saying to newspaper reporters as he went,
'Don't these guys know that the election is over?' The people

refused, however, to take that as a final answer, and such was their discipline and persistence that within a month the mayor was back, listening to the issues, and from that meeting changes began to be made in the life of that part of the city.

We have visited such broad-based communities in Harlem and Brooklyn and not only have we seen the huge new housing co-operatives built on urban wastelands of Brooklyn where previously the city council had insisted that nothing could be done, but also, equally impressively, we have seen the sparkle and confidence in the eyes of a black American woman in Harlem, showing us her community with pride, witnessing to the changes she and her congregation had been able to make, and thrilled with the fact that professional black Americans were now choosing to move back into Harlem because of its culture and community life.

We like the story of the group of Indian women gathered together by a community organizer in one of the townships of Madras. They came from several different faith-groups but they had one thing in common: they were tired of seeing their husbands coming home drunk at the end of the week, having spent most of their earnings on alcohol. They decided that, above all, they wanted their community to be a sober community where the little money available was spent on family life and not on alcohol. They decided to act together. Whenever a man came home drunk he would be surrounded by a group of women mocking him. Most of the men being harassed in this way would flee in confusion and only return when they were sober. The life of the township was transformed, and out of this basic victory the women went on to tackle issues such as education and health. Nor was their religious faith neglected. Following one of the 'actions' they met together in different faith-groups, Hindu, Muslim, Christian, etc., and sought to draw out of their faith-tradition what it was that made a 'good community'. They then shared their insights with the other faith-groups, not to seek any 'faith lowest common denominator' but to give one another confidence that in working to build a good community they were being true to the teachings of their faith.

But perhaps the most surprising and impressive advocate for Broad-Based Community Organizing was the director of an extremely wealthy trust on the edge of Wall Street. When we finally made it through security guards, secretaries and aides to his office, and he realized that we were not asking for money but information, he shared eloquently his belief that the 'seed-corn' money which his trust has put into funding the early life of broad-based community groups has brought better return in terms of changed lives and communities than any other funding programmes he knows. Broad-Based Community Organizing is now spreading to the cities of Africa and Britain. It is hard-headed, and perhaps manipulative of those in power. It does not appeal to every dedicated faith-filled person or community, but it challenges its detractors to find other methods equally effective in empowering the urban powerless.

The development of base communities having religious faith as their *raison d'être* brings a new understanding, which perhaps is merely a rediscovery of an old truth, that the faith-community is not only going with the grain of human nature, but is going with the grain of God. The biblical story is one of God calling people into relationship with one another and with himself. The people of Israel first emerge as a coherent people in covenant with God and with a developing self-understanding of their role of witnessing to God's holiness and righteousness before all nations. Then at the other side of the cross/resurrection experience we see the emergence of the Christian Church as a universal people of God empowered by the Holy Spirit to become a channel of grace through which the kingdom of heaven might come.

Clement of Alexandria used the word 'synergy' to describe the co-operative action of the human will and the grace of God.[6] The action depends upon the openness of the human will, no matter how poor and weak, to the grace of God all around. The loving, harmonious community we see in the Trinity of Father, Son and Spirit is characterized by openness and generosity, by the giving of the Son and later the Spirit to the world in love. The openness of a people to God leads not only to an uplift of the individual heart and soul before the beauty and holiness of divine love, but also to a co-operation of people with each other and with God's creative power in transforming the pain and ugliness of the world. The grace spilling over from the community of God the Holy Trinity, then, is the driving force which enables human community to be created and sustained.

There is a Christian folk story concerning the Holy Trinity.

Before the creation of anything at all, God the Father is living in perfect harmony and peace with God the Son, with the love of God the Holy Spirit flowing endlessly between them. It is a self-sufficient and self-sustaining community of peace and love. In the story God the Son says to his heavenly Father, 'This is wonderful but shouldn't we be sharing our community with others?' 'Do so,' says his Father, 'but it will cost you your life.' And it does.

This simple story carries in it three elements which we want to emphasize. First, that the basic Christian model of God is of persons living in community. Second, that it is of the nature of any true community that it must be shared. And third, that such sharing is costly. The whole of creation can be seen as the spilling over from the Trinity of the creative energy of God, and the faith-story of the Christian community culminating in the cross/resurrection story of Jesus can be seen as the cost of such sharing of community.

Religious community life is not easy. In Chapter two we discussed the vows of poverty, chastity and obedience which hold together the common life of the traditional religious community. Many people are attracted to the thought of 'giving their whole life to God' through joining such a religious community. The magic and the enthusiasm can ebb away after a few months or years, however, in the face of the hard realities of community life. A traditional community does not let initial enthusiasm lead people into a lifetime of regret. There are stages of commitment in community life. The new community member spends time as a postulant before becoming a novice, and only after several years as a novice are life vows allowed to be taken. At each stage the other community members are consulted before the new member deepens his or her commitment, because the life of the whole community is enriched or damaged by the presence of each of its members.

In today's world, of course, there are alternatives to the traditional Christian religious community; for example, enthusiastic religious seekers join Christian house churches and movements or become members of a Buddhist order. This may be wholesome and healthy for an individual spiritual pilgrim, but can be dangerous to them and their family members if the cautious checks and balances of the traditional religious community are missing. In our final chapter we indicate what can go wrong in community life when this balance is absent.

For most 'ordinary' people of faith, their religious community will be their local congregation. It is with them, over the years, that their faith is broadened and deepened. It is that community which shares the joy of significant events in life's journey and provides help, comfort and support during difficult and dark times. It is that community, with its total range of ages and its doors ever open to the wider community, which provides the religious and human 'extended family' where all have an honoured place and all have a contribution to make.

It is sometimes easier to see the value of this sort of religious community life by encountering the communities of another culture. Their experience holds up a mirror which enables us to see our own congregational life more clearly. The Japanese Anglican Church is a small community-based church and the community is real, powerful, devotional and committed to Christian discipleship. It has grown out of a long history of persecution and struggle. When we visited Japan as part of a group we were aware of the spirit-filled community from the moment we arrived at Narita Airport, to be met by a welcoming group from the Diocese of Yokohama, until the time when we were escorted back to the airport at the end of the visit.

The Japanese have the ability to live intensively, focusing upon what they see to be essential within the rituals and responsibilities of ordinary living. The mountain-based Christian family camp which we attended illustrated this. There, a large part of the family of the diocese was gathered for worship, fellowship, walks, music and talks. We had spent a long day travelling by train to the camp at Kyosato. We had then walked up the hill to the conference centre and were grateful to be met and given a packet of biscuits and a drink. We then assumed that we could quietly rest and get our bearings. Not at all. Our bags having been deposited, we returned to the main hall for a celebration of the Eucharist. The camp had started as it would go on, within an atmosphere of fellowship and devotion. An unbelievable variety of opportunities were packed into the two-day camp. There were barbecues, discussion groups, and a choice of walks, music and other activities. There was regular worship and celebration, and an opportunity to listen to traditional Japanese drumming.

Hospitality throughout our visit was painstaking and caring, our hosts meeting us on railway platforms, driving us around, returning our lost items and providing exactly the right refreshment at the right times.

It would be easy to see Japanese church life as unspectacular and even domesticated. That would be a mistake. It has grown out of a long tradition of persecution ever since missionary activity was forbidden in the late sixteenth century. Finally Christianity was banned altogether in 1637, so that torture and death followed a confession of faith. In the middle of the nineteenth century Japan became more open and missionaries began to return. It was then discovered that Christians had continued to live their faith secretly throughout all the centuries of persecution. We were taken to the Christian Museum at Oiso where we saw many reminders of the time of secrecy and suffering, including crosses hidden in carvings and crucifixes hidden in the backs of Buddhas. We were shown blocks of wood with relief carvings of Mary and Jesus. The pictures printed from these blocks were then used to detect hidden Christians, who were asked to step on to the prints and were killed if they refused.[7] The early paper prints were later replaced by bronze images.

At the Oiso Museum we were shown a wooden block with the figures of a mother and child without faces. It was explained that the Buddhist woodcarvers had produced the blocks without faces to help the Christians in their time of trial, because they need not avoid treading on images without faces and so could save their lives.

The Japanese church is a community church, then, proud of its spiritual traditions and history and, as a small faith-community, determined not to be isolated in a ghetto from the rest of Japanese life, but rather to be a distinctive community within a community, at ease with people of other faiths and with people of no faith. The Christians have good relations with Buddhists and with the followers of the Shinto tradition. We were told of Matsuo Basho, a seventeenth-century Buddhist poet, who left home to wander in search of truth. We were taken to the Tsurugaoka Hachiman Shrine at Kamakura, where we met the high priest of Shintoism in Japan. We drank tea and ate rice biscuits at low tables and we discussed interfaith issues. We also met and shared in discussion with the head of the Pure Land Buddhist Centre, which has the famous huge bronze 'Daibutsu', the Buddha in Japan, called Amida, honoured by most Japanese Buddhists. We visited the So-ji Head Zen Buddhist Temple in Yokohama, a large and spacious working monastery.

In Japan, then, we encountered a community-based church which has grown strong in struggle, in the face of persecution, opposition and, more recently, of indifference. We encountered a church which works to be part of the wider community of other faiths and of no faith. We encountered a church which works for reconciliation with those outside Japan who suffered in World War II. We know of at least one Englishman who was a Japanese prisoner of war and worked on the Thailand railway. When he went to stay with his son in Japan after the death of his wife, he found himself part of a loving and caring church where he was comforted in his bereavement and at the same time healed of his alienation from the Japanese.

There is great interest in the Japanese church in the story of Vivian Redlich, the English missionary priest who was beheaded on a beach by the Japanese in Papua New Guinea in 1942. When the church in Papua New Guinea celebrated fifty years since the death of Vivian Redlitch and other missionaries they did so with fifteen Japanese Christians, one of them the Anglican Archbishop, who were there in friendship and in sorrow for the past history which made the occasion necessary. Vivian Redlich's family home was at Little Bowden, near Market Harborough, where his father was the parish priest. When a service was held in Leicester Cathedral in his memory, the Bishop of Yokohama sent a representative to the service, with a letter which read, 'I would like to express our regretful sorrow for your sad memories of the past history . . . in Papua New Guinea and other Southern Pacific areas where Father Vivian Redlich and his fiancée and other people were killed by the violence of the Japanese soldiers . . . As a Japanese I confess our deep sorrow . . . and I am asking for your friendly benevolence to forgive our past . . . Hoping to deepen our future mutual understandings and friendship . . . ' It seemed a long way for the Japanese priest to come for the service, but his simple presence and the reading out of the letter transformed the occasion into one of understanding, reconciliation, and hope for future living and working together.

The Japanese Christians are not alone in discovering that sometimes when a community is threatened with attack or beaten, divided and exiled its spirit may stubbornly flourish and its people may become most spirit-filled, most powerfully aware of being a community – provided it believes in itself, its right to exist, and its future. The Bishop of Lebombo, Dinis Sengulane, travelled constantly throughout his country during the long Mozambique war, meeting people and providing the link of community in a time of near-despair. Everywhere he went he had a very simple way of helping people to feel that they still mattered, that they had a future and that ordinary times would return. When he visited the village people, before leaving them he planted a row of potatoes and promised them, 'I will be back for the harvest – and by then peace will be nearer.'

Another people whose faith has enabled them to live through times of great suffering and emerge triumphant are those who live on the island of Barbados. They do not forget their past, indeed whenever we go to Barbados we are made aware of the shameful history of the coming of the majority of the people to the island through slavery. And yet that history does not become a source of bitterness and resentment, but has been transformed into a new and joyful way of life. For example, the Crop Over Festival, which used simply to mark the end of the sugar harvest and therefore a pause in the suffering and death of harvest time in the plantation, now exists in a new guise. Part of the Crop Over which flourishes today is the calypso festival, and we have enjoyed the colourful calypso evenings when serious issues are raised in a light and humorous way. We have heard songs on relationships, on family life and its problems, on drug problems and on Aids. The development of calypso was one way in which the oppressed slaves of the past retained their humanity and developed the spirituality which continues in many of their descendants. Through the calypso the slaves were able to express themselves freely on the problems they were facing, and this was allowed because it was done seemingly light-heartedly and for entertainment.[8] But the community had found its way not only of surviving but of handling its problems, hopes and dreams, within a faith-filled community life.

An individual cut off from both homeland and home community can feel hopeless and helpless even when living in what seem like comfortable surroundings. A friend wrote the story of a Palestinian Arab living in exile in the West, who 'yearned continually for the land, the olive trees, the village, his daily life. He had hoped to make a new beginning, but he lacked the vigour or the desire to do so. Slowly he began to die.'[9]

But the community can be a source of new life and hope even in exile. William Saroyan wrote of the Armenian people:

I should like to see any power of the world destroy this race, this small tribe of unimportant people, whose wars have all been fought and lost, whose structures have crumbled, literature is unread, music is unheard, and prayers are no more answered. Go ahead, destroy Armenia. See if you can do it. Send them into the desert without bread or water. Burn their homes and churches. Then see if they will not laugh, sing and pray again. For when two of them meet anywhere in the world, see if they will not create a new Armenia.[10]

We live in times when two seemingly conflicting trends press upon community life. As we have seen, ease of transport and communication brings a new sense of global society and culture, consolidated through the growth of multinational companies and markets where goods, finance and services wing around the world. Perhaps in reaction to this is the sense of local tradition and heritage and a desire to hold fast to distinctive cultures and understandings. The challenge of community-building in our time, then, is to harness this basic and natural desire for small group, tribe or national identity to the need to develop a sense of global neighbourliness which will enable us to co-operate in building civilization and caring for a fragile and limited world. The same challenge is true for faith-communities – harnessing respect for the various religious faiths which have brought and continue to bring meaning and purpose to local people and communities, in a world where the faiths now encounter one another and overlap, positively in dialogue but dangerously in conflict.

We would like to give three examples where we have observed this sense of global neighbourliness being developed within an attitude of profound respect for the local. We recently visited the United Nations Headquarters in New York on a Saturday morning. We joined the groups being shown around and they themselves were made up of a large number of different cultures and nationalities. The guides had obviously been chosen from different nationalities and emphasized that, although the building happened to be located in New York, we were standing on international ground. Not surprisingly there was little sense of world unity for us in the great Assembly debating chamber because it was quite empty, but as we wandered around the building, images of world culture appeared, rather like snapshots from a global tour: a Viking ship donated by Norway; a beautiful woven carpet from the Middle East; exquisite ivory carvings from the Far East. Our group showed a polite interest in these and other artefacts, thanked the guide for the tour, and then scuttled down to the gift shop in the basement where the Western cultural contribution – glossy and glitzy souvenirs of all descriptions – was avidly snapped up to be taken back to homes around the globe. We wondered whether this was a parable of our time – a beautiful building, created around a silent global debating chamber – appropriately silent perhaps because humankind today has no overall vision or philosophy and is getting tired of the shout of debate? The building contains frozen images honouring local cultures, but the artefacts which are being purchased and spread around are the new, the brash, the disposable.

Are faith communities faring any better? We were privileged to attend a large interfaith gathering in Bangalore in 1993, which marked the centenary of the first World Parliament of Religions. It would be foolish to claim that the participants accurately represented the life of faith around the globe; some faiths were more represented than others, and those people who attended were mostly self-selected and so were likely to be predisposed to interfaith dialogue and co-operation. Speaker after speaker emphasized the unity of the spiritual quest, and the same vision of spiritual unity permeated the discussion groups. Yet the way in which the talks and discussions went forward eloquently illustrated the different insights and under-standings of the major world faiths, and these differences became even more clear as visits were made to the various temples, churches and mosques of Bangalore. We learned once more that respect for truth must lie at the heart of interfaith community building: respect for the distinctive truth of the other faith, but an equal respect for the distinctive truth of one's own faith. Dietrich Bonhoeffer taught the Church that there was no such thing as 'cheap grace'; we are beginning to learn that although chauvinistic faith-postures are no more attractive than their nationalistic equivalents, 'cheap inter-faith dialogue' which avoids hard questions is of limited value.

Institutions, political or religious, however, can only go so far in building global community whilst respecting the distinctive nature of local community. The United Nations, the World Council of Churches, a World Parliament of Faiths, may have their part to play, but they must be complemented by direct human experience where individual people can meet and talk face to face with those of different nations, cultures and faiths, and this can best be done within the small group situation.

To some extent, this happens quite naturally. Britain today is multicultural and we have opportunities of faith and cultural dialogue on our very doorstep. Other people travel around the world with their work and so have the opportunity of immersing themselves in different cultures, although more commonly they move from one international hotel in the West to an identical international hotel at the other side of the globe.

Many people have benefited, however, from the additional opportunity of going with a group from Britain and sharing for a few weeks the life of a church or faith-group in another country and culture. Through the work of Christians Aware, for example, we have seen how individuals from Britain have had their faith and understanding transformed through living and working with faith-groups in Kenya, India, Sri Lanka, Egypt or the West Indies. And because community-building today must be from everywhere to everywhere, equal benefits have emerged from groups from these countries joining with church or community groups in Britain as they engage in local community building. A sense of neighbourliness balancing the claims and needs of global and local community building can be achieved. It requires a certain openness, risk and even hard work, but that is the theme of the next chapter.

NOTES

1. P. Lewis, *Islamic Britain* (I. B. Tauris, London, 1994).
2. Adi Granth, 1242.

3. J. L. Segundo, *The Community Called Church* (Gill and Macmillan, Dublin, 1980).
4. R. Rezende, *Rio Maria – Song of the Earth* (Orbis Books, New York, 1994).
5. M. Grundy, *Light in the City* (Canterbury Press, Norwich, 1990).
6. A monk of the Eastern Church, *Orthodox Spirituality* (SPCK, London, 1978).
7. S. Endo, *Silence* (Penguin, Harmondsworth, 1988).
8. K. Davies, *Emancipation Still Comin'* (Orbis Books, New York, 1990).
9. N. Farah, *Colour of Courage* (Christians Aware, Leicester, 1991).
10. Quoted in *What Lies Ahead? Listening to Refugees* (Christians Aware, Leicester, 1991).

CHAPTER EIGHT

Sacred Work

'IF WORK was so great, the rich would have monopolized it long ago.' So said Mark Twain, suggesting that the benefits of work were not all that they were sometimes made out to be. Albert Camus would have disagreed with him, however. He wrote, 'Without work all life goes rotten', and this has been the general belief of social reformers. Perhaps the most well-known book castigating the evils of unemployment was George Orwell's *The Road to Wigan Pier*. In it Orwell, writing in the 1930s, spoke of the evils of a society which produced streets where 'nobody has a job and where getting a job seems about as probable as owning an aeroplane'.[1]

In recent years the West, affected by the world recession, has seen unemployment returning in some places to the levels of the 1930s. The result has been to turn Mark Twain's axiom on its head – where work is scarce, the rich have monopolized it. And so we have seen some people working frantically all hours of the day and sometimes into the night to cope with the volume of work coming their way, for fear that if they turn any work away the opportunity might not come again, because they are well aware that other folk, often no less talented or qualified than themselves, can find no work to do.

This polarization extends wider than the individual to households and communities. Because one member of a household is in work, he or she has contacts into work opportunities, sometimes casual or part-time, which can be put the way of partner or child. So living next door to one another will be 'work-rich' households, where every member is in work, and 'work-poor' households, where nobody has a job. We seem to be moving rapidly to a form of society where those in permanent work are a relatively small but highly-skilled élite who will be given high rewards and prestige over against a growing body of those with casual or no employment, who exist on a basic social wage and in the grey world of moon-lighting and even petty crime.

The polarization extends to societies. Those communities formed around a single industry such as mining see their whole work-base collapse with the collapse of the core industry. The traditional skills of the community, however highly developed, are not such as to attract new concerns looking for different and often lesser skills. And traditional craftsmen with years of pride in their craft are not usually the easiest people to retrain for skills that they inwardly despise, particularly when they are still grieving for the loss of a loved industry and way of life.

Social philosophers and reformers, then, are ambivalent regarding the nature of work. Is work a necessary evil or the right of every able-bodied man and woman? If 'the devil finds work for idle hands to do', does a society which cannot or will not provide work for all its members risk disintegrating, particularly when those without work come disproportionately from the young male members of ethnic minorities (which has tended to be the case in the West in recent years)? And if a society risks becoming sick if all its members are not in work, what of the effect on the health of the individual?

Medical experts have their own insights. Richard Smith, the editor of the *British Medical Journal*, wrote:

The physical health of the unemployed tends to deteriorate, and they are likely to visit their doctors more often – particularly with chronic cardio-vascular conditions. But it is mental health that is most harmed by unemployment. The unemployed experience anxiety, depression, neurotic disorders, poor self-esteem, and disturbed sleep patterns, and they are more likely than the employed not only to kill themselves but also to injure them-selves deliberately. The psychological damage stems mainly from loss – of status, purpose, social contacts, income, and a sense of belonging and mattering, but unemployment also brings stigma, humiliation, and a reduced scope for making decisions.[2]

Of course all this trauma at the loss of work may simply be a demonstration that modern Western society has elevated work to the level of an idol. If the first question we ask of a stranger, having ascertained his or her name, is 'What do you do?', then naturally the answer 'I'm unemployed' is likely to carry with it pain, humiliation and anger, unless the person comes from a profession such as acting where unemployment tends to be the norm rather than the exception. Even there, however, polite convention encourages the use of the word 'resting' rather than 'unemployed'.

If social philosophers, reformers, politicians and doctors have differing insights regarding the role and value of work, particularly where work is in short supply, what of those approaching work from the perspective of religious faith? Again the positions are many and varied.

It is often thought that the greatest polarization regarding work is between the different religious traditions of East and West. The wandering Hindu monk would teach that the world is a trap, even imprisonment; he would say, 'As a great flower turns from the world and faces the sun, so I would keep my back to the world and my face to God.' That might be the ultimate ideal for those called to be a monk but in fact Hinduism has a healthy common-sense approach to life and recognizes that not everybody can be a monk. The Hindu tradition is actually very balanced and even permissive in the way it sees people working and living in the world and at the same time approaching God. There is no ultimate 'right' way to God. The 'active' person serves God through work and duty; the 'emotional' person through devotion to a personal God in worship and prayer; the 'intellectual' person through the pursuit of knowledge and truth; the 'reflective' person through meditation and mind control. The various schools of Yoga are available to help disciples of the various ways: Kriya Yoga – preparation; Hatha Yoga – control of the body; Karma Yoga – service and duty; Raja Yoga – the yoga of the mind; Mantra Yoga – the use of repetitive phrases in meditation; Gnani Yoga – the pursuit of wisdom; and Bhakti Yoga – the yoga of loving devotion.

In thoughts echoed in Shakespeare's seven ages of man, Hinduism speaks of the individual's lifetime being first pupil or student, then soldier, then householder, spouse and parent. Then begins the withdrawal from world and work, first as devotee and finally, having renounced all, as sage or wandering ascetic monk. In this teaching there is a proper place for work, though prayer, meditation, and contemplation are the final goals. Hindu philosophers have not always marked such a clear progression or such clear divisions, but have made work in the world and worship of God two sides of the same coin, enhancing each other, or even two facets of the same picture.

One statue stands out for us from the many fine sculptures in the grounds of Shantiniketan, north of Calcutta, the perhaps unique campus of the university founded by Rabindranath Tagore in 1921 as a place of excellence in the arts for people from all over the world. It is the statue of a student by Ram Kinkar Beij, but Nanda Lal Bose has added a bowl of cooked rice to the head of the student so that it has also become a portrayal of Sujata, who took rice to the Buddha whilst he was meditating and thus in a direct and practical way entered into his spiritual quest.

A student with a bowl of rice to give in service of another conveys the whole, wholesome and even holy message that work and worship go together, they cannot realistically be separated. Vivekananda, a disciple of Ramakrishna, might be called the first Hindu missionary to the West. He attended and spoke at the first World Parliament of Religions in 1893 and set up the Ramakrishna Mission and the Vedanta Societies in Europe and America. He appealed for people to live whole, wholesome and holy lives, and challenged them to do this by linking meditation and study to disinterested service for and with people in the world. He challenged people to 'go from one part of the country to another, from village to village, and make the people understand that mere sitting about idly won't do any more.'[3] Vivekananda saw service as service of God, for he saw God in the people and believed therefore that there was no dichotomy between sacred and secular or between contemplation and action. He saw no danger of people forgetting God in the middle of a crowded programme of work, so long as they developed a constant awareness of God in all things and all people. He suggested three stages for the spiritual aspirant: 'work and worship'; 'work as worship'; and 'work is worship'. He taught that the three stages could be tackled by both monastic and lay people, even whilst they were in the middle of their working lives, so long as they worked towards strength, detachment, unselfishness and an uninterrupted focusing on God.

In the second chapter of the *Bhagavad Gita* Krishna advises
Arjuna to see God as partner in the battle of life, to work with
God for the sake of the work itself, without selfish desire:

But thou hast only the right to work, but none of the fruit thereof: Let not
then the fruit of thy action be thy motive; nor yet be thou enamoured of
inaction.

Perform all thy actions with mind concentrated on the Divine, renouncing
attachment and looking upon success and failure with an equal eye.
Spirituality implies equanimity.

Vivekananda's appeal for contemplation and action, for work
as worship, was taken up by other philosophers including
Mahatma Gandhi. He taught that it was a mistake to separate
religion from the world because the world itself is sacred –
every flower, every drop of water, every cow, every animal,
every person. He saw it as his mission to 'imbibe politics,
religion, business and family life with spiritual values'. And he
lived as he taught. A visitor came to him and asked him to teach
him meditation. 'Of course,' said Gandhi, 'Come at 4.30 a.m.
and join me at my meditations.' The man got up early and
arrived full of keenness to learn methods of prayer. He found
Gandhi hard at work clearing up the night soil from around the
well. Along with this approach came, naturally, a transformed
understanding of work as worship – no meditative methods,
no exercises, but people working with their hands rather than
sitting in lotus postures. 'Simple living, high thinking' was
Gandhi's motto, with work the centre of significance because
'the brain would be nothing without the thumb'.[4] He rarely
used the word 'spirituality'. He would say, 'Water your roots
with labour and suffering, then spirituality is the aroma of the
flower which others will notice.' The life of his ashram was
arranged around these principles, but although work was
central and sacred there was no worship of work. No member
was required to work for more than four hours a day. In this
balance between work and worship the Gandhian communities
were similar to the Christian monastic community first formed
and forged by St Benedict in the sixth century.

Gandhi would have approved of the Jewish story of the hard-
working cobbler. The cobbler went to Rabbi Isaac of Ger and
asked him what he should do about his morning prayers which

tended to be squeezed out by his work, mending the shoes of poor people. As he explained, the people depended upon their shoes to go to work, but as they had only one pair each they could not work until the shoes were mended. The Rabbi asked the cobbler, 'What have you been doing until now?' The cobbler explained that sometimes he rushed through the prayer very quickly and then rushed back to his work, feeling guilty. Sometimes, however, he missed the prayer-time altogether and felt a great sense of loss, and every now and then sighed 'What an unlucky man I am, that I am not able to make my morning prayer.' The Rabbi said to the cobbler, 'If I were God I would value that sigh more than the prayer.'[5]

The biblical attitude to work is polarized around two theological insights which have partly contributed to the everyday attitudes with which we began this chapter. Firstly, work ought to be a dignified process whereby humans co-operate with God in the stewardship and development of his creation. Secondly, because of humankind's pride and rebellion humanity has become enslaved by work. It has become a curse and a toil so that, far from ennobling human beings, work degrades and dehumanizes them.

In the New Testament itself the world of work forms much of the stuff of Jesus' parables and suggests that the ordinary world of work was part of his way of life and that of his hearers. Work may be an important part of living and the common-sense wisdom of business, farming, shepherding, fishing and stewarding may provide insights when responding to the coming challenges of God – such is Jesus' teaching in the gospels, and he goes on to indicate that, important though work may be, it should not be got out of proportion. So the fact that a man had just bought a pair of oxen and was naturally eager to yoke them up and test them was no reason for him to rudely set aside the invitation to attend the kingly banquet of the kingdom of heaven. The claims of God come before all human claims, including those of work.

The teaching of St Paul that 'Those who don't work shouldn't eat' (2 Thess 3.10) must be seen as wise, practical, down-to-earth advice to new Christians who mostly did not come from the higher strata of society. It must also be seen within the context of the Greek and Roman world which was greatly

influenced by the presence of slavery. Work was a subordinate
activity performed by subordinates. Work in order to earn a
wage was demeaning. Work was likely to preoccupy and
degrade the mind. A higher calling was to use leisure well.
'Those who don't work shouldn't eat' was Paul's instruction to
any Christians tempted to adopt such a philosophy.

It was the rise of the monastic movement which led once
more to a serious consideration of the place of work within
creation and salvation. As we have said, perhaps the most
influential development in community life in the Christian
tradition was made by St Benedict. In the Rule of St Benedict
work takes its natural place alongside worship, prayer and
community life. Worship is work, and work is worship. Every
member of the community works and there is no first- and
second-class work – manual toil is just as significant and just
as holy as mental toil, and every member of a community
is expected to do both. There is no place for individual pride
or gain through work, because all is done for, and with, the
community. All work must be approached in a humble, patient
and loving way, with awareness of God's own presence and
work.

The Benedictine practice of putting work and worship
together on an equal level, interdependent and interrelating,
was the ideal, but it has to be admitted that the early vision
and practice were always having to be recreated by, for
example, the Cistercians, as 'worldly' aspirations and ambitions
permeated even to the heart of such set-apart communities. And
if these Western communities were perhaps contributors to
Vivekananda's teaching and Gandhi's practical balance between
work and worship, they did not have the same vision of the
sacredness of ordinary life outside the monastic community.
Indeed their taken-for-granted notion was more like that of
the Hindu holy man – the 'first-class' spiritual life was to be
found as a monk or nun, and the 'ideal' Christian life was to be
found in the monastery or convent. Those who could not aspire
to this must do the best they could as 'second-class' Christians
working in the world and bringing up the family.

For an early Western understanding of God centrally present
in ordinary life and work we must turn to a Celtic understanding which was overshadowed but not destroyed by Rome from

the seventh century onwards. Many of the early Celtic crosses have scenes from the Bible on one side and scenes from everyday life on the other side; there was no division. Many of the early prayers and poems of the Celtic people were collected and written down by Alexander Carmichael in Scotland and by others in Ireland at the end of the nineteenth century. The prayers were clearly prayed by people who saw no separation between their work and God's loving kindness towards them. The prayers are natural and simple and they were, and still are, prayed to Father, Son and Holy Spirit, who are believed to be with the workers throughout the day and the night. Some of the prayers are prayed in the trust that Christ and sometimes Mary and other saints are joining in the work of cooking, farming and fishing. There is a fine collection of prayers about lighting the fire in the morning. One of them begins, 'I will kindle my fire this morning, in the presence of the holy angels of heaven.'[6] Going to bed at night also produced comforting prayers: 'I lie down this night with God, And God will lie down with me.'

The Celtic understanding of God with the people in their everyday living and working is not unlike the strand in Hinduism which produced thinkers like Vivekananda and Gandhi. One story of St Bride is that she had poor parents. There was a terrible drought and little Bride was asked to look after the house whilst her parents went out to look for food. She was left behind with a small stoup of water and a bannock of bread. She was told to be very careful with her supplies and to let no one into the house. Two strangers called towards evening. One was an old man, with brown hair and a grey beard, the other was a beautiful young woman. They asked for a place to rest. Bride shared her water and the bannock between them. She had to obey her parents so she could not let them into the house, but she felt sorry for them. She showed them around to the stable at the back of the house. When she returned to the house the bannock was whole and the water stoup was full. When she went out she saw a brilliant light all golden over the stable door, for the Christ had come.

A CELTIC RUNE OF HOSPITALITY USED BY
THE IONA COMMUNITY

> I saw a stranger at yestere'en
> I put food in the eating place
> Drink in the drinking place
> Music in the listening place
> And in the Name of the Sacred Three
> He blessed myself and my house
> My cattle and my dear ones
> And the lark said in her song
> Often, often, often,
> Goes the Christ in stranger's guise
> Often, often, often,
> Goes the Christ in stranger's guise.
>   Kenneth Macleod[7]

Many of the world faiths have stories of God coming to earth in disguise. Hinduism has many such stories. Vivekananda and Gandhi, like Mother Teresa, saw God in the faces of the poor and saw service of the poor and needy as the greatest work, the service of God. They were inspired by the verses from the *Bhagavad Gita*, 'Whatever thou doest, whatever thou dost eat, whatever thou dost sacrifice and give, whatever austerities thou practisest, do all as an offering to me.'[8] In the Christian tradition Jesus challenged his disciples to work for the poor and needy, his brothers and sisters, and to do so realizing that any work of kindness was an act of kindness to himself, Jesus, to the Christ: 'I was hungry and you fed me, thirsty and you gave me a drink; I was a stranger and you received me in your homes, naked and you clothed me; I was sick and you took care of me, in prison and you visited me' (Matt 25.35–36).

The Reformation, together with technological and social change, brought the challenges of Christ more obviously into the lives of the ordinary people of Europe. The vernacular Bible and Caxton's printing press made it possible for a Bible to be possessed and understood by the new class of educated merchant. No longer were ordinary working folk dependent upon the industry of pen-wielding monks to produce the Bible, or the scholarship of other-worldly priests to translate and expound it, not always in the most comprehensible or accurate way.

Martin Luther's German translation of the Bible was lively and even homely, so that people could easily understand it and remember it, and even sometimes act upon it of their own volition. Luther's hymn, 'A safe stronghold our God is still',[9] is not unlike the much earlier Celtic prayers and songs, including St Patrick's prayer:

> Christ be near at either hand,
> Christ behind, before me stand
> Christ with me where'er I go
> Christ around, above, below.[10]

In England Cranmer produced a vernacular liturgy – a round of prayer modelled on the sevenfold office of the monastery but built around a daily pattern of Morning and Evening Prayer which was meant to be used by everybody in their local parish church. The division between the 'professional' holy person in the monastery and the 'second-class' Christian at daily work had gone.

This revolution in church thinking and practice resonated with social change. New professions and trades were appearing with their own organizations, so that now community was to be found not only in palace, monastery or home, but in the workplace, trade and profession. Work was not merely a way of earning a living for self and family, it had become a vehicle for companionship, loyalty, trust, status, education, initiation, social and community care.

Before long the theology caught up with the reality. If work was so significant in the life of people and the community, then it must have a significance in the sight of God. The Puritans came up with a theological explanation of this significance. They taught that work is not just a necessary evil, or a way of ordering society, it is part and parcel of the scheme of salvation. Through the life and death of Jesus God had made possible people's salvation. The response was faith in Jesus and then 'working out salvation' in daily work. Faithful work in the world, then, was seen as a response in gratitude for the gift of salvation. So the 'Puritan work ethic' was born and on it were built banking and commercial empires – Barclay's, Cadbury's, Rowntree's and the rest.

By the early nineteenth century in Europe success in work was

seen by many Christians as the reward from God for living well
and for working hard, and the result was a general philosophy
that hard-working, responsible but possessive individualism was
the way to live, a philosophy that saw a resurgence in the 1980s,
especially in Britain and America. According to this philosophy,
the labouring poor of the countryside and, increasingly, the
urban poor who were normally hidden away in factories and
coal-mines were poor either because they did not work hard
enough or because they were ordained by God to be so. The
factories of the nineteenth century brought great wealth to their
owners, but not everyone was blind to the social consequences
for those who fed the engine of production. One song of the
period was 'The Factory Bell', which told how,

> Here at the mills in pressing crowds,
> The high built chimneys puff black clouds,
> And – all around the slaves do dwell,
> Who're called to labour by a bell.[11]

People, including children, still exist in similar conditions
around the world today in many countries where labour is
cheap. The organization Anti-Slavery International brings to the
attention of those in our society willing to look the plight of the
many children who work long hours in the fields, on family
farms, on farms owned by others, or on plantations. Others
work in urban backstreet sweat-shops or factories. More often
than not, this means exhausting, unhealthy and dangerous
labour. Still others get caught up into criminal activities or child
prostitution. The 'slaves are still dwelling', but now they are
further away![12]

By the mid-nineteenth century individualistic philosophy
and theology were being challenged by a few pioneers. In the
Church of England a group arose which set itself to work for
co-operation in place of competition in every aspect of life.
The Christian Socialists, especially F. D. Maurice, one of the
founding fathers, based their work upon their belief that Christ
had come for all people, and was in all people, not just those
who called themselves Christians. Nothing was outside God's
sphere. They set about their work on political, economic and
social issues with the support of the doctrine of the incarnation,
which a group of them wrote about in *Lux Mundi*, published

in 1889.[13] Christ's coming to the earth had highlighted the value of the material world and of every person in it. 'Let the working men of England claim their rights as Christ's members and do their duty as Christ's soldiers and the present order would crumble,' said Stewart Headlam of the radical Guild of St Matthew.[14] The same year, 1889, also saw the foundation of the Christian Social Union with Bishop Westcott as founding president. The CSU campaigned against sweated industries and influenced the Trade Boards Act of 1909 which set up machinery for fixing minimum wages in industries where the workers were scattered and poor, whilst one of the national chairmen of the Church Socialist League, founded in 1906, Lewis Donaldson, wrote that both Christianity and Socialism required 'pity for the weak, justice for the oppressed, the . . . sanctity of life . . . and fellowship instead of competition as the dominant method in industry'.[15]

The cry was taken forward into the twentieth century and well beyond the shores of Europe, by groups like the Cambridge Mission to Delhi founded by Bishop Westcott, which in the 1990s, as the Delhi Brotherhood, is going from strength to strength in serving and enabling the poor. We have visited thriving communities of leprosy patients who are building new lives for themselves and their families, in farming and craft-work like spinning and weaving. Frank Weston, the Bishop of Zanzibar, who had been a student member of the Guild of St Matthew, took up the torch of Christian Socialism in 1923 when he addressed the Anglo-Catholic Congress and said,

You cannot claim to worship Jesus in the Tabernacle if you do not pity Jesus in the slum . . . It is folly – it is madness – to suppose that you can worship Jesus in the Sacraments and Jesus on the Throne of glory, when you are sweating him in the souls and bodies of his children.[16]

The Church in Tanzania had an excellent foundation for the development work which has been a significant part of its mission activity throughout the twentieth century.

Lewis Donaldson initiated a permanent record of his belief that the struggling and competitive world, the direct cause of suffering amongst the poor, could only be changed when people began to recognize themselves as part of a family. He planned a series of paintings for the sanctuary of his parish church of St

Mark in Leicester, where he attracted working men to attend church and from which he shared the leadership of a march of unemployed people to London in 1905, thus raising awareness of a national as well as a local problem. The march was later recognized as having great influence on the social legislation of the Liberal Government in its years of office. The artist of the paintings was Eadie Read, and they were dedicated in June 1910. The main theme to be developed was 'The Travail and Tragedy of Labour', caused by the organization of society for the pursuit of riches instead of the common good, a degrading situation for all people even though it was the poor who suffered. Christ came to demonstrate the possibility of redeeming labour by love and sacrifice, so that it could become a free service, a true vocation where all, performing different functions, could be one in Christ himself.[17]

In many different religious traditions, then, and at different times in history, work has been transformed when it has been regarded as vocation. A similar message comes from a surprising source, the film *Zulu*, frequently shown on TV. It is set in South Africa and tells the story of an engineering officer who, with his platoon of soldiers, was sent way out into the bush to build a bridge across a river. Whilst they were doing just that, building their bridge, the Zulu War started and they were under attack. The officer had an unexpected load of care to carry – the defence of his men. His responsibility soon grew, for there were other soldiers in the area, fighting men, but because our hero was the senior man, he was called to take overall command. So the defence of the whole area was his responsibility, and he had a load of care which he had not sought but could not avoid. We see him ruefully saying to his young second-in-command, 'You know, I only came here to build a bridge.'

Soon civilians arrived, missionaries, traders, all gathering for protection. Men, women and children came and made their homes in the makeshift camp. The officer's family of care expanded and as he strolled around the camp late one night, viewing his charges, the film shows him muttering to himself, 'I only came here to build a bridge.' Then the war started in earnest. The Zulus attacked in wave after wave, a sea of warriors. Many of the soldiers were killed, others fought on bravely, using their parade-ground tactics, trusting in the skill and experience of their commanding officer. In a lull between attacks, whilst his men regrouped and his assistant tended his wounds, the officer complained bitterly to his God, 'I only came here to build a bridge.'

Finally it seemed that all was lost. The Zulus grouped for a final attack but then, astonishingly, instead of pressing home their advantage they formed up and saluted the soldiers for their bravery and withdrew, leaving the commanding officer smiling with relief, and saying, 'I only came here to build a bridge.'

Our hero only came to build a bridge and he found that he had a war on his hands. He had to weld unfamiliar soldiers into a fighting force. He had to defend squabbling civilians. He had to inspire his men to bravery and comfort them in their pain. He had to remember long-forgotten lessons from the parade-ground. He had to accept defeat and victory calmly and graciously. A load of care had come unexpectedly out of the blue, a load which he had not looked for but could not avoid, and that load of care had expanded. He only came to build a bridge but he was called to organize a war, and through his faithfulness to that call many lives were saved.

Vocation is often so. The call comes out of the blue as a load of care. The load expands, but through a faithful response lives are transformed. It is possible to see the same pattern in the story of Jesus from Nazareth. We see him first as a young boy, sitting at the feet of the scholars, asking them intelligent questions. Next, we see him as a young man, caught up into the renewal movement of Judaism headed by John the Baptist. Care for God and his coming kingdom had caught him and would never let him go. That care drove him into the desert where he wrestled with diabolical temptations. It drove him on to the hillside where his followers were caught up into his vision of a transformed future. They sat at his feet as, like a new Moses, he expounded the new law of a new way of life. 'Blessed are the poor in spirit; blessed are the peacemakers; blessed are those who hunger and thirst after righteousness.' Blessed, because life in the coming kingdom would be transformed, the dreams of those who knew their need would be fulfilled.

It was a beautiful vision, but his ministry of shouldering God's load of care did not turn out to be quite so straightforward. His

natural supporters, the good pious churchmen and women of
the day, turned deaf ears and blind eyes to his message. They had
better things to do with their lives than risk them in foolish
ways. But the poor, the bad, the indifferent, those who knew
their need responded, and before long Jesus snapped at those
good churchmen and women, 'I have not come to call the
righteous but sinners.'

So his load of care had expanded. He had only come to
renew Judaism and he had the lost sheep of the house of Israel
on his hands. But his care expanded still more, for as he
wandered outside the borders of Israel he met foreigners whose
faith astonished him – Samaritans, Romans, Gentiles of all
description were soon claiming his attention and love. So not
only the lost sheep of the house of Israel but also the lost
Gentiles of the world were embraced by his love and care, and
as he rode into Jerusalem on Palm Sunday it seemed that the
whole world was cheering him.

Then the mood changed. The cheers turned to jeers and
the load of care expanded in quite a different direction:
to the agony of Gethsemane; to the betrayal by his friends; to
the condemnation by the Jewish faith he had come to renew;
to the execution by the state which he would have transformed.
The prince of peace had become the saviour of sinners. The
saviour of sinners had become the rejected, crucified, helpless
scapegoat of the world, with the future of his mission hidden in
the mysterious darkness of God. Then the crucified Jesus of
Nazareth became the triumphant Christ of the Church – risen,
ascended, glorified – whose gospel of hope and love embraced
the globe and stained every corner of a wounded world. For
Jesus too, then, the call of vocation, the load of care came out
of the blue and caught him. As he shouldered that load of care
it expanded until it filled the whole universe, and through his
faithfulness lives in every age have been transformed.

We see the same pattern of vocation emerging in women and
men of our own age – a load of care coming out of the blue
and expanding, then through a faithful response lives being
transformed. For example, during a recent trip to Japan we
visited the Elizabeth Sanders Home near Yokohama. Who was
Elizabeth Sanders and what is her home? In the years of
American Occupation following the end of the war a number

of illegitimate children fathered by GIs were born to Japanese girls. These children, hated as a sign of Japan's humiliation and defeat, were often abandoned at birth by their distraught mothers. A certain Japanese aristocrat, Miki Sawada, was introduced to this situation in a dramatic way. She was travelling by train one day when the train swept around a corner and a parcel fell on her head from the luggage rack. To her horror she found that the parcel contained the corpse of a newly-born 'mixed-race' baby.

Care for these pathetic abandoned babies grabbed Miki Sawada out of the blue and would not let her go. Nobody was interested in the problem. Indeed they were embarrassed even to discuss it. Miki was relentless. She begged land, money, and resources to open a home for the abandoned babies, and then she named it after Elizabeth Sanders, an ordinary English school-teacher, who had left a modest amount of money for the project in her will. In the early years it was a tremendous struggle to establish the home, keep it open, staff it and raise the money to feed the children. And the need never grew less, though its nature changed. Today the home is a well-established and respected complex of buildings housing dozens of children, from toddlers to teenagers. Hundreds of children, now grown men and women, have cause to be grateful for the faithfulness of Miki Sawada.

A similar story of vocation coming out of the blue, grabbing, growing, and transforming lives, could be told of a former Surrey schoolteacher, Joyce Pearce. In 1951 whilst the rest of the country was celebrating the Festival of Britain, Joyce invited seventeen 'displaced' East European teenagers to spend a holiday at 'Ockenden', her Woking home. The visit was a tremendous success, with the group being almost smothered by the hospitality of Woking people. In particular they valued the contact with local teenagers, and friendships were begun which have continued ever since.

The project turned Joyce into a world traveller with a compelling concern for the plight of the young homeless refugee. She first visited Germany to see at first hand the conditions in the refugee camps from which her young visitors had come. On her return to England she began lobbying English schools to offer more refugee children hospitality, and as more and more schools did so, she also established a pattern of 'Ockenden

Weekends' where the children could come and keep in contact with one another. Finance was always a problem but Joyce's motto was, 'If there is a need, there must be a way.'

Soon 'Ockenden Homes' were springing up all over the country and, as they did, the load of care expanded in a different direction – Tibet. Following an uprising of Tibetans in 1959 against the Chinese invaders, ten thousand people were killed in three days. The Dalai Lama and thousands of his people escaped, amongst them many hundreds of unaccompanied children. Joyce Pearce was persuaded that the Ockenden expertise was needed in Asia and off she went to tour the Tibetan settlements in India. As a result she wrote a detailed report for UNICEF, and on her return to England managed to raise sufficient funds to establish 'The House of Faith' for Tibetan refugee children. And so the story goes on: an orphanage in Saigon; an ashram in East Bengal; a purpose-built school for girls in the Sahara; a refuge for Afghan refugees in Pakistan; project after project bringing aid, comfort and hope to hundreds of fractured young lives. In 1984 Joyce died of cancer, but the work goes on, in the Ockenden Venture, and what a legacy – countless lives enriched by her faithfulness in shouldering an expanding load of care over forty years – a vivid example of true vocation, sacred work.[18]

We finish with a powerful Buddhist story which encapsulates for us the nature of vocation.[19] The story concerns a bandit who one day murdered a significant citizen. He then lost no time in fleeing away as fast and as far as he could. He travelled across lake and land by boat and horse, stealing a jewel here, a silver candlestick there, to raise money to pay for his transport and lodging. But by so doing he left behind a trail that the son of his victim, who had sworn to avenge his father's death, would painstakingly follow.

The bandit realized that he would never be safe from revenge until he could leave the country and start a new life elsewhere. But to do that he had to cross a mountain range and he had to do so quickly for soon winter would be closing in and the track across the mountain would be impassable. Many other folk had the same idea and he joined the straggling line of travellers as they followed the track which climbed and meandered towards the shoulder of the mountain. After climbing for some thousands of feet, the track narrowed to a thin path which eventually became a scar scratched across a precipice. As the bandit reached this spot he saw a group of frightened travellers huddling together, watching as a young man with burdens on his back edged his way forward a step at a time.

Impatiently the bandit pushed forward but as he did so the young man slipped and began to fall. The bandit grasped his arm and pulled him back to safety. The bandit then began to curse the travellers, saying, 'What kind of fools are you to travel so sure a way to death?' But they told him that there was no other way. They said that the cost of the cheapest boat around the mountain was far beyond their means. They told him that unless they crossed the mountain they would be living in abject poverty. Even whilst they spoke another party was coming up. There was only one thing to do. The bandit went down into the village and bought rope and brought it to the precipice. Securing one end here, he edged to the far side and secured the other end there. Day after day he went up the mountain to the precipice and with the help of the rope enabled the children and the elderly to cross the dangerous ravine.

One day he had the misfortune to be ill and whilst he lay on his sick-bed two travellers slipped to their deaths. He could see only one solution if the battle with the mountain was to be permanently won – a tunnel. He bought a pick, climbed up to the ledge, and drove it into the rocky mountainside with all his strength and hate and love and yearning. Before long the people of the village below had adopted him as a kind of local saint. He rarely left his lengthening tunnel now but the villagers brought him food and water to keep up his strength.

Meanwhile the son of his victim was following his tracks and finally reached the region where the bandit was at work. When still many villages away the young man heard of the tunnel. He was interested but did not relate it to his mission. It was some time before he realized that the saint and his quarry were one and the same person, but even then he simply believed that pseudo-sainthood was merely the bandit's way of escaping retribution. 'It will not work', he grimly told himself. He would have his revenge, and in a delicious way.

He packed food, took a boat and travelled around the mountain. Then he returned to his home and started calculating – ten years. 'I will return in ten years and kill him, an inch before he breaks through.' He was true to his word, and ten years to the day he was back at the village, now famous in all the land as 'the village of the digging saint'. But the avenger had under-estimated the severity of the task, for he was told the tunnel would not be completed for another year at least.

His curiosity got the better of him and he climbed up the mountain to get a glimpse of his prey. He crept into the tunnel and despite himself he was overawed at the enormity of the task which the bandit had almost completed. And then he saw his victim, a giant of a man, and the bandit/saint instinctively knew who he was and why he was there. The young man drew out his sword. 'Now,' said the big man, 'You haven't waited so long to kill me without a fight. I promise you, we will have our duel, but not until the tunnel is finished.' So saying he turned and calmly got on with his work.

Day after day the young man returned to the tunnel to measure progress and hurl insults at the big man. Soon, because he was no longer welcome in the village, he, like the saint, camped in the tunnel itself. One day as the big man was trying to roll a huge boulder to the tunnel's mouth the young man found himself standing shoulder to shoulder with his enemy, pushing the boulder with all his might. It took them half a day, then that evening the young man went down and bought his own pick, telling himself that the quicker the work was completed the sooner his father would be avenged.

From that day forward the two combatants worked together, mostly in silence, sometimes in fury, occasionally with a feeling of companionship. One day, after months of work, the big man told the young man, 'Tomorrow we will be through and you can have your fight.' The young man found himself weeping uncontrollably. The big man put his hand on his shoulder and whispered, 'You must do it. It's only your hate that has kept you going for fifteen years. It is all you have.'

At midday the big man's pick broke through. In a frenzy he ripped and stretched the hole until it was wide enough for them to see out. They looked down. The tunnel ended in the face of a cliff higher, steeper, wider and more deadly even than that at the other end. They stared. The big man pulled back and pressed against the wall and murmured, 'I was so sure of the direction. But that's it. I've finished.'

The young man whispered, 'We can't stop now. Come on, we'll extend the tunnel in the correct direction. I'll work with you, perhaps it won't take that long.' The big man walked to his sword. 'No, if you want to fight, then fight now, otherwise I'm leaving.' The young voice was loud with anger, 'You can't go. I can't finish this alone. It's not my work.' But the big man was already striding towards the light, calling over his shoulder, 'It's not mine. No more. It's all yours.' His footsteps receded down the passage.

The bandit, the murderer, seeking escape, found himself with a load of care, unlooked for but unavoidable, which tied him to the land. The young man, his father's avenger, nurturing a great hate and a great task – revenge – found, unlooked for and unwanted, companionship; found a new and different task, the tunnel; and found that he had inherited a great load of care. His only decision was whether or not to own it. Both men found themselves caring profoundly for tasks which they had not sought but which called and held them. Such is the nature of vocation – sacred work.

NOTES

1. G. Orwell, *The Road to Wigan Pier* (Penguin, Harmondsworth, 1983).
2. R. Smith, 'Without work all life goes rotten', *BMJ* (1992), Vol. 305.
3. Swami Vivekananda, *India and Her Problems*.
4. M. Chatterjee, *Gandhi's Religious Thought* (Macmillan, London, 1983).
5. Anthony de Mello, *The Prayer of the Frog* (Gujarat Sahitya Prakash, 1987).
6. E. de Waal (ed.), *The Celtic Vision. Selections from the Carmina Gaedelica* (Darton, Longman and Todd, London, 1990).
7. D. Adam, *The Cry of the Deer* (Triangle, London, 1987), p. 26.
8. *Bhagavad Gita – the Gospel of the Lord Sri Krishna*, trans. Sri Purohit Swami (Faber and Faber, London, 1978), Chapter 9.
9. M. Luther, 'A safe stronghold our God is still', in *Hymns Ancient and Modern, New Standard* (Hymns Ancient and Modern, Norwich, 1983).
10. D. Adam, *The Edge of Glory* (Triangle, London, 1989), p. 91.
11. R. Palmer (ed.), *Poverty Knock* (Cambridge University Press, Cambridge, 1974).
12. Anti-slavery International, 180 Brixton Road, London.
13. *Lux Mundi*, ed. C. Gore (John Murray, London, 1909).

14. M. B. Reckitt, *Maurice to Temple* (Faber and Faber, London, 1946).
15. B. J. Butler, 'Frederick Lewis Donaldson and the Christian Socialist Movement' (unpublished thesis, Leeds University, 1970).
16. H. Maynard-Smith, *Frank, Bishop of Zanzibar, 1871–1924* (SPCK, London, 1926).
17. B. J. Butler, 'Frederick Lewis Donaldson and the Christian Socialist Movement.'
18. P. Watkin, *Joyce's Ockenden* (Broadmead Paperback, 1993).
19. W. D. Jennings, *The Ronin* (Charles E. Tuttle, Rutland, VT, 1968).

CHAPTER NINE

'Sacred Bovines!'

The mystic was back from the desert.
'Tell us,' they said, 'what God is like.'

But how could he ever tell them
what he had experienced in his heart?
Can God be put into words?

He finally gave them a formula
– so inaccurate, so inadequate –
in the hope that some of them might be tempted
to experience it for themselves.

They seized upon the formula.
They made it a sacred text.
They imposed it on others as a holy belief.
They went to great pains to spread it in foreign lands.
Some gave their lives for it.

The mystic was sad.
It might have been better if he had said nothing.

Anthony de Mello[1]

We hope that we have been able to communicate some of the excitement we feel about the spiritual quest, and the variety of ways in which different human cultures and individuals have encountered the divine. But it would be wrong not to admit that spirituality can have its dark shadow, often caused by the pursuit or worship of 'sacred bovines', or more crudely 'sacred cows'.

James Gleick, an American journalist, wrote a popular book on chaos. He was then the recipient of a number of earnest letters from all over the world: from Tokyo, 'This is a letter proposing a new model of the world – a duoverse'; from Texas,

'I've notified two universities but have received no response. I can clear up the confusion in quantum physics'; from Prague, 'I am the first in the world as to the number of the found arithmetic progressions of prime numbers. Will you please send to me $500,000'; from California, 'I have come up with a chemical–biblical equation (some fifty-two pages long) which outlines or explains the difference between a well-ordered universe and the universe which exists today.' Mr Gleick's correspondence is not dissimilar to a proportion of the post-bag of anybody at all involved in public life. The letters tend to have common threads. There is the belief that the writer is the possessor of a great truth. There is a somewhat lonely feeling of rejection. 'I have written to government ministers, professors, bishops and the Queen, but nobody takes me seriously.' There is an obsession with a single 'truth', which will revolutionize the way we understand the world.

Now it cannot be denied that occasionally a person has come up with such a truth. Albert Einstein revolutionized modern physics whilst sitting quietly in his dull patent office and asking himself, 'What would the universe look like to me if I were riding on a beam of light?' From that question the theory of relativity was born which, together with the discovery of quantum mechanics, has brought totally new insights to our study of the universe. When asked how he managed to make his discovery, Einstein answered, 'I continued to ask the questions that children ask.' It cannot be denied, then, that although human discoveries usually emerge from the painstaking work of knowledgeable people working in teams, breakthroughs can occur in more dramatic ways and this encourages those who feel that they themselves have been the recipients of such a truth.

But there is a second consequence of the recent progress of modern science. The picture of the universe given us by relativity and quantum mechanics is decidedly odd or even bizarre to the common-sense mind. It is not surprising, therefore, if otherwise intelligent people feel free to believe in a whole variety of notions. Some, like ESP or parapsychology, are pseudo-scientific; some, such as channelling and the healing power of crystals, have a more mystical feel. Certainly the 'New Age' section of most bookshops dwarfs the science or the mainline religious sections. The science writer Martin Gardner summed all this up over a decade ago by saying, 'Our nation is now in the midst of unprecedented enthusiasm for beliefs that medieval astronomers would have considered insane.'[2] Perhaps this enables us to understand a little the happenings at Waco, Texas.

In April 1993 in Waco, Texas, some eighty people from the Branch Davidian sect, a fundamentalist community started by David Koresh, barricaded themselves into their Mount Carmel headquarters with an arsenal of weapons including 350 guns and two million rounds of ammunition. After a fifty-one-day siege they were mown down in the ensuing battle with US law officers, and died in the flames or found themselves facing criminal charges. A video filmed inside the building just before the final attack gives us a flavour of the community. David Koresh is nursing gunshot wounds and is also nursing one of the forty-six children of the community. He is quoting scripture! The events at Waco reminded us uncomfortably of the mass suicide which took place a few years earlier in the Guyanan jungle, when some nine hundred people who had gathered around the Revd Jim Jones met together for a final ceremony. They gave their children orange juice laced with cyanide, and then took the poison themselves, lay down and died.

But it is the conflagration of the members of the Order of the Solar Temple in Switzerland in July 1994 which gives us the best insight into the mindset of those caught up into such sects. Fifty-three people died. They were apparently stable, sensible individuals from France, Canada, Britain and Switzerland, pillars of their local communities. Yet they believed that they were reincarnated members of the medieval order of knights and that to escape the coming apocalypse their leader would one day soon take them on a journey to the planet Sirius where it was thought certain Lords of the Universe dwelt. The elements of the cult included the communication of a 'secret wisdom' through occult rituals, combined with elements of mysticism and mythology surrounding UFOs. The leader of the cult was a 69-year-old successful businessman, but to his disciples he was 'The Great One', reincarnated from the ancient sect of 'The Rose and the Cross' which controlled the destiny of humankind.

Disciples would come from their ordinary mundane lives as farmers, travel agents, nurses or handymen and don elaborate crusader-style capes, enter a chapel in the basement of a Swiss chalet and get caught up in an intoxicating mixture of myth, mystery and magic. All this might seem weird but harmless play-acting, yet it led to murder and mass suicide. Why? How is it that seemingly normal people again and again get caught up into fundamentalist sects and become so committed to them that they would rather die than set the myth aside?

We believe that the desire for certainty lies at the heart of the attraction of such sects. Any religious cult which promises certainty seems to find eager followers. Why? Well, if you pound people hard enough with certainty when they are feeling vulnerable under the pressures of life; if you offer them instant family when their lives are poor in friendship; if you offer them a message which makes meaning of life, when their lives are confused and problematical; if you offer them a special task – to spread the group's gospel – when their work is dull or meaningless, or they can find no work to do; if you offer them clear leadership when they can find no one to admire or believe in or follow in their world or church; if you offer all this, together with intoxicating, mind-numbing worship – then you are offering a powerful package which many people will buy. Andrew Malcolm, a Toronto psychiatrist (several Solar Temple Members came from Toronto), has written,

Many people find the great imponderable questions of life unbearable. They need concrete, clear-cut answers to existential problems like what comes after death, and what is the fate of the world. There is no simpler solution than a messianic cult with a programme where all followers will be saved and reassembled on the other side of time, after the apocalypse.[3]

The attraction of the cults, then, is to offer clear, simple answers to complex human questions. The answers are offered within a framework of tight community life united behind a charismatic leader.

The psychological danger of this is obvious. It is a sad truth that mystical insight and mad illusion seem to lie close together in the human psyche. The great religions have always known this and have their checks and balances through worship, prayer and pastoral care so that people can get in touch with the reality of God without destroying themselves in the process. A religion can and should bring holiness and goodness to the lives of its followers, but the religious impulse when out of control can become a dangerous drug, and in the hands of an unscrupulous leader it can be a menace. People caught up in such a pseudo-religious movement are deeply suspicious of the world outside, which they often believe to be in the grip of the devil. They are drawn into an ever-deeper dependence upon the belief system of the sect. They are incapable of seeing reason; they are too busy seeing visions.

The psychological danger is obvious, then, but there is an equally real theological danger. It is not too ridiculous to claim that the lust for certainty is the original human sin. In the story in Genesis the forbidden fruit in the garden which archetypal humans were forbidden to eat was the tree of the knowledge of good and evil. Eat it and you would be like gods. Eat it and you would have certainty – eat it and everything would become clear. A religious or political leader offering the fruit of certainty will always have followers, who sometimes will follow him or her to their deaths. It is disturbing that so many people have terrible doubts about religion today, but it is even more disturbing that so many have terrible certainties.

Heresy is a word much out of favour today. But in past ages heretics were simply extremely keen Christians who had often seized upon what was true but then, by giving it exclusive importance and by losing sight of other balancing truths, promoted it in a way which was distorting, misleading and even destructive. Such heresy lies at the heart of much cult teaching. It is impossible to doubt the sincerity of those caught up in such teachings. For example, it has been estimated that it takes some four thousand hours of knocking on doors in Britain to make one convert, but the fanatical gleam in the eye of the doorstep evangelist and the simplistic world-view being portrayed make it seem that such a person is literally 'not all there'. He or she is excluding too much about life and the world which we know to be true, because if such truths were also to be accommodated the whole dogmatic package of utter certainty would become unravelled.

There is an animal, the bamboo lemur, whose eating habits are so specialized that it can eat bamboo (the pith of which is laced with cyanide), because its stomach produces a chemical which is an antidote to the poison. The price it pays is that it cannot eat anything else. If the bamboo goes, so does the lemur. Cult members might thrive for a while on the diet of specialized belief which is on offer, but others are not usually tempted to follow their example, for they rightly see that such a narrow perspective is poisonous to the human spirit.

We believe that the confusion between certainty and faith is crucial to understanding the lure of fundamentalist sects. St Paul reminded the Christians in Corinth (who were always ready to make exciting rabbit-runs down blind alleys), 'Now we see in a mirror dimly, but then face to face. Now I know in part; then I shall understand fully' (1 Cor 13.12). The writer of the Epistle to the Hebrews states, 'Now faith is the assurance of things hoped for, the conviction of things not seen' (Heb 11). It is noteworthy that he uses practically-orientated words, 'assurance', 'conviction', not philosophical ones such as 'certainty' or 'knowledge' to describe the confidence we need to walk with God. In any resilient faith which gives its followers the opportunity of spiritual growth, there is a necessary tension between a practical working confidence and metaphysical certainty. For faith is not certainty, it is a way of living creatively without certainty.

The offering of certainty in the realm of the spirit, then, is one of the sacred cows on offer today, but there are other sacred cattle on hand. Some groups claim authenticity for their doctrines by offering direct mystical experiences. There has always been a certain caution in the great faiths towards such experiences, partly because there has not been any obvious connection between the experiences and holiness of life, and it is the latter which religious faith seeks to encourage. There is a story of St Theresa, who was interrupted one day by a novice nun who told her with great excitement that she had just had a wonderful vision of heaven, 'Never mind, my dear,' the great saint said. 'Get back to your work and prayer and I am sure that it will soon go away.' With the drug culture of the 1960s and 1970s producing mind-blowing experiences in people foolish enough to dabble, we can perhaps see why the great mystics have refused to regard visions and the like as being of any great spiritual importance. What matters is the journey of trustful faith, and because faith is 'seeing dimly through a glass in this life', one should expect to meet the 'dark night of the soul' as much as any comforting vision, and one should not be blown off course or overly impressed by either.

The computer which holds our word processor also has a programme for playing chess. The board is presented on the screen, the user indicates a move and then the screen goes blank whilst the computer plans its response. At the easiest level this takes less than a second, but, as the user improves, the skill level increases and the screen is blank for a longer time whilst the computer 'thinks'. It would be easy to assume that nothing is happening during this 'thinking' time, because nothing can be seen, the screen is dark, but in fact a great deal is going on. The most important thing is that the user is gradually being taught greater and greater skill. That might be analogous to Christian mystics through the ages. It has been their experience that God is powerfully present, not in the bright, brief glimpses of illumination but in the 'dark night of the soul' when it seems that nothing very spiritual is going on, yet in fact that is where the faithful believer is being drawn along the path of holiness and true spirituality.

We have seen that the spiritual community can be of enormous significance to many people. The vision is that of the creation of a renewed part of the world where people can live simple lives together, loving one another and serving others. Such communities may be accompanied by a variety of lifestyles, perhaps basic farming methods, simple clothes and accommodation, communal meals, stylized names. We see an example of such a community in Iris Murdoch's novel, *The Bell*.[4] Why do such communities so often fail? Marghanita Laski, in her book *Everyday Ecstasy*,[5] provides an intriguing answer. She defines three sorts of people around the community, 'servants', 'counter-élite' and 'the enemy'. 'Servants' are the community members with the vision, and with the desire to serve the un-privileged 'counter-élite'. The 'counter-élite' may be extremely worthy, they may be those others find unattractive or even repulsive, or they may be a group, perhaps even a symbolic group, 'the workers', etc. 'The enemy' are those resistant to the vision and living ordinary, self-centred lives. The community fails partly because the 'counter-élite' tend to be more attracted to the values and possessions of 'the enemy', and because a number of the 'servants' eventually find that the magic of living vision-filled

lives wears off. So the community splits amidst mutual recrim-
inations. There is nothing wrong, of course, with the vision of
communities like this, in fact such people have often proved to
be those who have brought desirable changes to society. The
problem is that the vision which appeals to these community
members as the whole of life is to most people only part of life.
The other problem is that there seems to be no relationship
between the strength of a person's vision or commitment and
the worth of the vision itself. People can just as easily become
committed to a narrow fundamentalist sect as to a rich religion,
just as people can fall in love with a kind gracious person or one
who will make their lives a misery.

It seems that the test of a spirituality cannot therefore merely
be the strength of feeling of those following it, or the delightful-
ness of an experience, or the firmness of commitment to a
revealed 'truth'. Rather, the best approach would seem to be the
biblical test which Gamaliel brought to the early Church: 'by
your fruits you will know them'. Bishop Kirk came to the same
conclusion, 'Unless an alleged experience of God brings with it a
call to disinterested action of some kind or other . . . we shall
scarcely be able to avoid the conclusion that something is amiss.'

But it would be wrong to be too judgemental of those who
seem to be seeking certainty, chasing visions and dreaming
dreams. They are often trying to find people who share their
passion for religion in a society which is no longer excited by
the religious quest and which tends to regard those who are as
'religious nutters'.

We should have in mind the experience of one civil servant
commissioned to examine a particularly notorious new religious
movement widely believed to practise cannibalism, incest and
group sex. After interrogating some of the cult members, the
official, rather disappointed, reported:

It all amounted only to this, that on an appointed day they had been
accustomed to meet before daybreak, recite a hymn, and bind themselves
by an oath. After the conclusion of this ceremony it was their custom to
depart and meet again to take food . . . I found nothing dangerous, just
an extravagant superstition.[6]

The writer of that, the Roman governor Pliny, was describing
the life of the Christian church in Asia Minor in the first years

of the second century. Widely reviled and feared as a disruptive and exclusive sect, it grew under persecution and developed into an extensive and open world faith. It seems that we can safely leave the judgement of other people's spiritual journeys to God.

NOTES

1. D. Faivre (ed.), *Transcendence. Prayer of People of Faith* (Westminster Interfaith, London, 1994).
2. J. Gleick, 'Everybody has one theory in them', *The Daily Telegraph*, 6 August 1990.
3. 'The bonfire of insanity', *Sunday Times Magazine*, 29 January 1995.
4. I. Murdoch, *The Bell* (Penguin, Harmondsworth, 1962).
5. M. Laski, *Everyday Ecstasy* (Thames and Hudson, London, 1980).
6. Henry Bettenson, *Documents of the Christian Church* (Oxford University Press, Oxford, 1959), p. 3.